CATHARINE BEECHER

Catharine Beecher: The Complexity of Gender in Nineteenth-Century America investigates how the life of education reformer Catharine Beecher is a lens through which to understand the cultural changes of the nineteenth-century.

Catharine Beecher's writings outlined a unique domestic role for women just as urbanization and industrialization were limiting their social influence. By arguing that gender differences were a strength, Beecher empowered middle-class women to embrace domestic duties. This book contextualizes Beecher's life against the major changes that occurred during the first three-quarters of the nineteenth-century. By looking at Beecher's writings and anecdotes from her life, this book offers insight into her personality and how her career shaped the culture of femininity. Students and the general reader will find this a powerful and insightful introduction to Catharine Beecher, her work, and legacy.

About the Lives of American Women series: selected and edited by renowned women's historian Carol Berkin, these brief biographies are designed for use in undergraduate courses. Primary sources at the end of each biography reveal the subject's perspective in her own words. Study questions and an annotated bibliography support the student reader.

Cindy R. Lobel was an associate professor history at Lehman College, CUNY. She was the author of *Urban Appetites: Food and Culture in Nineteenth-Century New York* and an area editor and contributor to *Savoring Gotham: A Food Lover's Companion to New York City*. She was a specialist in urban history, food history, and culture in US history.

Laura J. Ping is an assistant professor at Bellarmine University. She is the author of "A Tale of Two Bloomer Costumes: What Mary Stickney's and Meriva Carpenter's Bloomers Reveal about Nineteenth-Century Dress Reform." She is at work on *Beyond Bloomers: Fashioning Change in Nineteenth-Century Dress*. Ping writes and teaches on fashion, social reform, and gender in US history.

Lives of American Women
Series editor: Carol Berkin

Selected and edited by renowned women's historian Carol Berkin, these brief, affordably priced biographies are designed for use in undergraduate courses. Rather than taking a comprehensive approach, each biography focuses instead on a particular aspect of a women's life that is emblematic of her time or made her a pivotal figure in her era. The emphasis is on a "good read," featuring accessible writing and compelling narratives, without sacrificing sound scholarship and academic integrity. Primary sources are included at the end of each biography, alongside study questions and an annotated bibliography, which support the student reader.

Julia Lathrop
Social Service and Progressive Government
Miriam Cohen

Mary Pickford
Women, Film, and Selling Girlhood
Kathey Feeley

Elizabeth Gurley Flynn
Modern American Revolutionary
Lara Vapnek

Dorothea Lange, Documentary Photography, and Twentieth-Century America
Reinventing Self and Nation
Carol Quirke

Catharine Beecher
The Complexity of Gender in Nineteenth-Century America
Cindy R. Lobel and Laura J. Ping

For more information about this series, please visit: https://www.routledge.com/Lives-of-American-Women/book-series/LIVESAMWOMEN

CATHARINE BEECHER

The Complexity of Gender in Nineteenth-Century America

Cindy R. Lobel and Laura J. Ping

Routledge
Taylor & Francis Group
NEW YORK AND LONDON

Designed cover image: Photograph of Catharine Beecher, public domain, held by the Schlesinger Library, Radcliffe Institute, Harvard University

First published 2023
by Routledge
605 Third Avenue, New York, NY 10158

and by Routledge
4 Park Square, Milton Park, Abingdon, Oxon, OX14 4RN

Routledge is an imprint of the Taylor & Francis Group, an informa business

© 2023 Taylor & Francis

The right of Cindy R. Lobel and Laura J. Ping to be identified as authors of this work has been asserted in accordance with sections 77 and 78 of the Copyright, Designs and Patents Act 1988.

All rights reserved. No part of this book may be reprinted or reproduced or utilized in any form or by any electronic, mechanical, or other means, now known or hereafter invented, including photocopying and recording, or in any information storage or retrieval system, without permission in writing from the publishers.

Trademark notice: Product or corporate names may be trademarks or registered trademarks, and are used only for identification and explanation without intent to infringe.

Library of Congress Cataloging-in-Publication Data
Names: Lobel, Cindy R., author. | Ping, Laura J., author.
Title: Catharine Beecher : the complexity of gender in nineteenth-century America / Cindy R. Lobel and Laura J. Ping.
Description: New York, NY : Routledge, 2023. | Series: Lives of American women | Includes bibliographical references and index. |
Identifiers: LCCN 2022027720 (print) | LCCN 2022027721 (ebook) | ISBN 9781032387581 (hardback) | ISBN 9780813348315 (paperback) | ISBN 9781003346647 (ebook)
Subjects: LCSH: Beecher, Catharine Esther, 1800-1878. | Women--Education--United States--History--19th century. | Sex role--United States--History--19th century. | Women--United States--History--19th century.
Classification: LCC LA2317.B35 L63 2023 (print) | LCC LA2317.B35 (ebook) | DDC 370.92 [B]--dc23/eng/20220718
LC record available at https://lccn.loc.gov/2022027720
LC ebook record available at https://lccn.loc.gov/2022027721

ISBN: 978-1-032-38758-1 (hbk)
ISBN: 978-0-813-34831-5 (pbk)
ISBN: 978-1-003-34664-7 (ebk)

DOI: 10.4324/b23305

Typeset in Bembo
by SPi Technologies India Pvt Ltd (Straive)

In Memory of Cindy Lobel

CONTENTS

Acknowledgments ix
Series Editor Introduction xi

   Introduction 1

1 Early Life 5

2 Beecher's Career Begins 18

3 Out West 28

4 Beecher's Conservativism 41

5 Domesticity 57

6 Education Reform 67

7 The Professionalization of Womanhood 82

8 The Final Phase 98

   Epilogue 117

Primary Sources 120
Study Questions 125
Bibliography 126
Index 131

ACKNOWLEDGMENTS

In 2010, Carol Berkin asked me to visit her home in Guilford, Connecticut. I was a first-year graduate student and new to the East Coast, so I was thrilled for the opportunity to explore New England. As we walked through the streets of Guilford admiring the colonial homes, Carol stopped in front a particular house with a plaque on the front. The dedication noted that the home had once belonged to Lyman Beecher, father of Henry Ward Beecher and Harriet Beecher Stowe. Catharine Beecher's name was missing. Carol and I both noted the exclusion. That day has stuck in my mind. At the time I knew of Beecher only as an education reformer, but as an aspiring historian I was keenly aware that when women's lives do not fit the mold they are often left out of the historical narrative.

When I began writing my dissertation a few years later, I once again became aware of Catharine Beecher. This time it was as a physical education advocate. Beecher's writings fascinated me both for their traditionalism and their radicalism. She argued that a woman's true calling was as a wife and mother. Yet she pushed against the status quo by urging these same women to embrace physical strength through exercise. I was intrigued. I knew my friend Cindy Lobel was writing a book on Catharine Beecher and I consulted her as I read through Beecher's writings. Catharine Beecher, Cindy told me, was full of such contradictions.

When Cindy asked me to co-write *Catharine Beecher: The Complexity of Gender in Nineteenth-Century America* I was honored. Beecher's life story resonated with me; she was a woman who used education as a tool to develop her own understanding of gender, separate from the teachings of her conservative childhood. It was also a joy to work with Cindy, one of the finest researchers and writers I have ever met.

Cindy's contribution to this book was invaluable and I know that she would have liked to thank her friends and family for all of their support. First, Carol Berkin, a cherished mentor and friend who made this book possible. Cindy's history cohort: Angelo Angelis, Phil Pappas, Peter Vellon, Megan Elias, Kathleen Feeley, and her colleagues at Lehman College. As we all know, books are never simply the work of one person, it takes a community. Cindy's husband Peter Kafka, who was always her biggest fan. Her sons, Benjamin and Jonah, the greatest joys in her life. Her mother, Kaaren Lobel whose encouragement meant everything to Cindy. And Cindy's closest friends, her sisters Jodi Lobel, Susan Lobel, and Debbie Lobel. Cindy came from a strong family, whose love inspired her to "include women in the sequel."

I would also like to thank Cindy for the opportunity to work on this book. My signposting has improved. I would like to thank Carol Berkin for her mentorship and for the chance to contribute to this project. Carol's patience and expertise makes me a better scholar. Thank you to my own history cohort: Megan Elias, Kathleen Feeley, Jenny Thigpen, Trish Stewart, Einav Rabinovitch-Fox, Sarah Gold McBride, Sandra Dawson, and Cecelia Hartsell for always cheering me on. I would like to thank my friend and cousin Jaime Brzuskiewicz for always making me smile. Thank you to Rachel Samuels for always being there and for making me take walks even when I didn't want to. Thank you to Maureen Kindilien for the long talks after a busy workday. Most of all, I would like to thank my husband, Jeremy Ping, for listening while I work through my ideas and always reminding me to take a big breath. You're my favorite.

LAURA J. PING
New York City

SERIES EDITOR INTRODUCTION

The nineteenth-century saw a number of remarkable women reformers and pathbreakers, including abolitionists like Sojourner Truth and Angelina Grimke, feminist theorists like Sarah Grimke, institutional reformers like Dorothea Dix, woman's rights activists like Elizabeth Cady Stanton and Lucy Stone, authors like Harriet Beecher Stowe, and women entrepreneurs like Madam C. J. Walker—to name only a few. But perhaps the most widely known woman of the century was Catharine Beecher. Celebrated by many, criticized by an equal number, this member of the notable Beecher family became the leading voice shaping American ideas of women's domestic role.

Beecher grew up in a family already well known for its celebrity. Her father, Lyman Beecher was a prime mover of the religious revival known as the Second Great Awakening, a movement that helped spur the country's first age of reform. While some of Lyman Beecher's children became advocates of abolition and women's rights, his daughter Catharine endorsed natural gender differences, insisting they were a strength for women as long as they devoted their energies to domestic duties and eschewed involvement in politics and public policy. She early on advocated the reforming and revitalization of American education, arguing that women's only legitimate civic role was to teach and educate the children of her nation. To prepare for this role, Beecher declared, women themselves must be well educated and trained. This conviction echoed the views of eighteenth century post-Revolutionary thinkers like Judith Sargent Murray and Benjamin Rush. But because Beecher was a doer not just a theorist, she established model schools of education for women. Her Harford Female Seminary embodied her vision of female education.

Beecher's fame, however, rested on her books and essays advancing her conservative views on gender roles. Women's place, she argued, was in the home.

When radicals like the Grimke sisters spoke out on political issues, Beecher engaged in a heated debate with them; women, she said, should never directly participate in politics. In 1841, she began to write steadily on what she considered women's appropriate roles. Her *Treatise on Domestic Economy* became the bible of the nineteenth-century's cult of domesticity; it served as a powerful challenge to the demand for female political, legal, and social equality that led to the Seneca Falls Convention. Later, beginning with *True Remedy for the Wrongs of Women*, she proposed that women's domestic duties should themselves be treated as professional positions (an argument soon echoed in the home economics movement).

Like many dominant figures in American culture and thought, Beecher herself was a living contradiction. A fierce advocate of domesticity, she never married, and remained economically independent. A bold reformer in education, she frequently abandoned the schools she established. Physically fragile and often suffering mental depression and exhaustion, Beecher was a fierce advocate of physical exercise for both sexes. Despite her own conservatism, she remained close to her brother—an avid supporter of abolition and women's rights—and to her sister Harriet, whose book condemning slavery influenced Abraham Lincoln and intensified the sectional tensions that led to the Civil War.

This book places Beecher's life in the context of her times. The nineteenth-century was a century of economic growth that prompted a shift from an agrarian society to an industrial power. It saw a revolution in communication and transportation, rapid urbanization, and a bloody civil war. These dramatic changes in American life led many citizens to advocate radical changes in racial and gender relations, but they also led many Americans to seek refuge in traditional ideas such as the immutable differences between men and women. Beecher spoke for those conservatives who believed public space belonged to men while the home and its children was women proper sphere. As we know, this debate over gender differences and gender roles continues today.

INTRODUCTION

In May of 1878, the Reverend Henry Ward Beecher offered a personal speech in his regular Friday night lecture at his Brooklyn church, Plymouth Church of the Pilgrims. The subject of that evening's speech: the life of his sister, Catharine Beecher, who lay on her deathbed at the age of seventy-eight. Reverend Beecher recollected his sister's "cheerful disposition," her assiduity in the face of a challenge, and her impact on American culture. As the *New York Times* reported on Beecher's remarks: "Few persons, even in the ministry, had influenced as many minds as she had," thanks to her work in education reform, her mentoring of teachers, and her writings on domesticity. Indeed, though she is relatively unknown today, Catharine Beecher was among the most famous and influential Americans in the nineteenth-century.

Catharine Beecher was born at a time when the concept of celebrity did not really exist. And yet, her family would spawn some of the most well-known Americans of the nineteenth-century. Her father, Lyman Beecher, was a fiery minister, who worked to spread the gospel throughout New England and the west. He raised eleven children (a twelfth died in infancy) and emphasized to all of them the importance of service to the Lord and community. The Beecher children embarked on extraordinary careers and the most famous of them devoted their lives to saving and reforming society. Beecher's sister, Harriet Beecher Stowe wrote the extremely popular and influential antislavery novel *Uncle Tom's Cabin*. Her younger brother Henry Ward Beecher became "the most famous man in America," gaining notoriety as one of the nation's foremost preachers and abolitionists and for his role in a sexual scandal with one of his parishioners. Beecher's half-sister Isabella Beecher Hooker became a leader of the movement for women's suffrage and cofounder of the National Woman's Suffrage Association. The less famous Beecher siblings were also involved in such reform movements as abolitionism and women's rights. Only one Beecher, Mary Beecher Perkins, remained aloof from the social reform movements of the age. She married and raised a family, including a daughter who would go on to parent the reformer, feminist theorist and author Charlotte Perkins Gilman.

Catharine Beecher's life spanned the nineteenth-century. She was born in 1800, into a new nation of 5 million inhabitants. These residents clustered within approximately 1,000 miles of the Eastern Seaboard. The nation's westward boundaries ended at the Mississippi River. The population of the United States was diverse for its time. It included people descended from various Northern European nations as well as Native Americans and 1 million people of African descent, most held in chattel slavery in both northern and Southern states. As Thomas Jefferson took office, the year of Beecher's birth, the agrarian economy and culture he believed best suited for a republic seemed to dominate. Ninety-five percent of Americans lived in rural areas. New York, the largest of the nation's cities, had a mere 60,000 inhabitants. Early industrialists were beginning to harness the power of water toward ironworks, textile production, and other manufacturing but the United States remained a rural nation, dependent on Europe, and especially England, for its manufactures.

It is almost unimaginable how different the United States was by the time of Beecher's death in 1878. The vastly expanded nation stretched from coast to coast. Its population of nearly 50 million included over 6 million immigrants, and 6.5 million people of African descent; none of them enslaved. The nation had emerged thirteen years before from a protracted Civil War, the deadliest war in its history and although it was still patching the wounds from that epic event, Reconstruction had ended, and the Southern states had fully re-entered the Union. Jefferson's agrarian dream had ceded unquestionably to an industrial nation, building a basis in corporate capitalism that would shape the nation's economy and culture inexorably.

The second half of the nineteenth-century was characterized by social unrest and division. The year before Beecher died, the largest strike in the nation's history had occurred, beginning with the railroad employees and evolving into a general strike. The Great Railroad Strike of 1877 showed the growing power of labor and the growing fissures between the people and the plutocrats that would shape both the Gilded Age and the Progressive Era that followed it. The nation's cities hosted the growth of corporate capitalism and the nation's rise into an industrial powerhouse. New York, the center of American finance and industry, claimed 1.2 million inhabitants (Brooklyn, then a separate city, housed almost 600,000 more). Chicago, which was a mere railroad junction in 1850 had reached a population of 500,000 and was poised to become the nation's second largest city by 1890. These cities were not anomalies; they pointed the way toward a rapidly urbanizing nation. One in four Americans lived in cities by 1880 and the culture of the city was spreading throughout the nation thanks to a national press and other media.

Catharine Beecher's life was shaped by and reflected these monumental developments. She had several careers—teacher, education reformer, author, domestic adviser, lecturer. Beecher's work took her from Hartford Connecticut to Cincinnati, Ohio, to Milwaukee, Wisconsin, and she crisscrossed the nation lecturing on education and domesticity Catharine Beecher was more conservative than her famous siblings Henry Ward Beecher and Harriet Beecher Stowe. Indeed, as the eldest Beecher, she diverged significantly from her brother and sister on the topics of female suffrage and abolitionism: she opposed both movements. But Beecher's views on women's education evolved over time. While still informed by Christianity, by the 1850s her lectures and writings no longer emphasized women's role as Christians or their national duty. Instead, she focused on how they could follow professions that emphasized and played on their natural role as nurturers.

Catharine Beecher's life thus serves as a window through which to see the major movements and developments of the nineteenth-century United States including industrialization, urbanization, women's rights, slavery and antislavery, national growth and westward expansion, the Second Great Awakening, Civil War and Reconstruction. More directly, Beecher's life shows us how gender mores and expectations, particularly for middle-class women, reflected and shaped larger national developments.

Catharine Beecher made a name for herself as one of the foremost advocates of both women's education and their domestic role. In both realms, Beecher emphasized what she believed were women's inherent differences from men and she sought to capitalize on these differences in order to carve out a role for women in American civil society. She thus took part in a long-running debate among American feminists over equality vs. difference in defining women's place in society. Even in the face of the monumental changes of the nineteenth-century, Beecher remained steadfast in her commitment to the differences between men and women.

Beecher is a complex figure, and her life represents the range of gender roles and experiences that defined white, middle-class women in the nineteenth-century. Within that range is a series of paradoxes. Catharine Beecher was one of the most famous American women of her time, but that fame did not rest on her family name, her father, or a husband. Instead, it was her own career and her own views that made Catharine Beecher a household name. Her books and essays crafted a powerful image of women's role as mothers and wives, protected from the very public sphere that Beecher, herself, inhabited as an author, lecturer, and educator. Indeed, while she was from a reformist, and in some cases radical family, in some ways Catharine Beecher bears a kinship to modern conservative women like Phyllis Schlafly and Sarah Palin.

Beecher was a pioneer of intellectual and physical education for women. She eschewed corsets, advocated calisthenics, and spoke out against the myth of female fragility. Yet, she also supported the notion that women's biological differences made them ill-suited for the rigors of the public sphere. And she suffered from mental and physical ailments throughout her life.

A supporter of women's superior role within the household and moral realm, Beecher opposed suffrage for women or any radical movements, including the abolitionist cause for which her famous siblings Harriet Beecher Stowe and Henry Ward Beecher became spokespersons. And, perhaps most interesting, this advocate of marriage and domesticity as women's natural and ordained role, never married or headed a household of her own.

Catharine Beecher was a member of an educated, white, northeastern family, and thus she was representative of a small slice of nineteenth-century American womanhood. We certainly cannot directly extrapolate from her experience that of middle-class African American women, or Native American women, or enslaved women, or immigrant women, or working-class women of any race. And yet Beecher *did* represent and advocate a very powerful model and ideal for all nineteenth-century women: the ideology of domesticity. This paradigm was at the heart of nineteenth-century American mainstream culture and society. And even though this ideal did not describe the reality of most women's lives, it exerted an important influence on the *expectations* of women's behavior and role.

Beecher serves as a symbolic bridge between two eras of gender conventions—the Republican Mother of the early national period and the municipal housekeeper of the Progressive Era. And she is part of a long trajectory in the history of American feminism between those who have sought equality with men by emphasizing similarities and those who have emphasized an elevated role for women in society and culture by concentrating on gender differences. By examining Catharine Beecher's life and works, this book will both use Beecher's life as a lens on the developments of nineteenth-century America and reflect on her place in the broad scope of women's and gender history.

Note

1 "Catherine (*sic*) Beecher Dying," *New York Times*, May 11, 1878, 5.

1
EARLY LIFE

When Catharine Beecher was born in September of 1800 the United States was still in its infancy. The American Revolution had officially ended only seventeen years before. Since then, the new nation was forging an independent identity, its leaders struggling with the task of governing a large and diverse country. The Constitution, ratified in 1789, strengthened the national government, but throughout the 1790s, fractious politics and political crises characterized this newly formed government. American leaders like Thomas Jefferson, John Adams, James Madison, and Alexander Hamilton debated the meaning of citizenship, the proper role of government, and the role their upstart nation would play in the world. Beecher was born just two months before the election of 1800 would anoint the Democratic-Republican Thomas Jefferson the President of the United States in a contested election against the sitting president, Federalist John Adams. The result was significant: a peaceful transition of power.

These national developments felt very far away to Reverend Lyman Beecher, meeting his first child for the first time in the remote hamlet of East Hampton, New York. But his hopes and expectations for this child went beyond the bounds of the nation. When his mother-in-law placed newborn Catharine in his arms, Lyman proclaimed her: "Thou little immortal."[1] In some respects, Beecher's assessment was correct. His eleven children amassed an impressive record as ministers, writers, and reformers, leaving an indelible mark on American society and culture. Catharine Beecher was at the front of this pack and in many ways her life both reflects and characterizes the massive social and cultural upheavals that the United States experienced over the course of the nineteenth-century.

The Beechers' East Hampton was a far cry from the tony beach community of today. Rugged, isolated, and sparsely populated with a mere 1,500 inhabitants, Lyman Beecher's first parish was literally and figuratively at the end of the earth.

The town had no store; goods had to be shipped in from New York City, which was 105 miles to the west, arriving each week on a schooner. The single road that ran through the town and toward the rest of Long Island was rudimentary and rutted. The town was accessed more easily by ferry from Connecticut than by road travel from the mainland, making East Hampton an offshoot of New England rather than New York City. Even travel to the nearest post office, seven miles away in Sag Harbor, involved an arduous journey, so communication with the outside world was difficult.

Lyman Beecher's parishioners, who made the trip on Sunday to his church from the towns around East Hampton—Amagansett, Accombomock, Three-Mile Harbor, the Springs, Fireplace, and Wainscott—were farmers and fishermen who did not venture far from their homes. Indeed, in his autobiography, Reverend Beecher surmised that "half the inhabitants of those retired villages made no other journey during their whole lives" than their Sunday trip to church.[2] Despite the isolation, he enjoyed working in the parish. He described his parishioners as "Industrious, hospitable [and] in the habit of being influenced by their minister."[3] The town had nary an infidel, sectarian, or even, to its minister's pleasure, a lawyer.

East Hampton was more typical of the communities of early national America than were the larger cities like New York, Philadelphia, or Boston. At the beginning of the nineteenth-century, 95 percent of Americans lived in rural areas and participated in a subsistence-plus economy, producing within the household many necessities such as candles, soap, clothing, and food, and purchasing or bartering for those items they could not produce. Among the goods to be purchased were tools, iron pots and pans, and luxury food items such as tea and sugar. Like Lyman Beecher's parishioners, most Americans existed in a proscribed sphere, never venturing more than a few miles from their homes. Most households had at least one servant; two indentured servants worked for the Beechers. Bonded to the Beechers until their twenty-first birthdays whereupon they would be freed, Zillah and Rachel served as nurses to the children. Artisans' households also included apprentices and, in some cases, unskilled laborers who worked alongside the master craftsman in his attached workshop.

When the Beechers lived in East Hampton, slavery was still legal in New York State. The gradual emancipation written into the state constitution during the American Revolution called for final manumission of enslaved New Yorkers in 1827. But most enslaved New Yorkers lived in cities or on farms, working in the fields, on the docks, and in artisans' workshops. The Beechers did not own slaves—they probably could not afford the purchase price—and the antislavery position for which the family would eventually become famous was already nascent in the Beecher home.

Lyman and Roxana Beecher had moved to East Hampton the year before Catharine was born so that Lyman could take up the pulpit of the town's Congregational Church. Lyman Beecher came directly from New Haven, where he had studied at Yale under the tutelage of Calvinist Minister and college President Timothy Dwight. Like his mentor, Beecher believed that conversion—a process by which one recognizes and abandons his or her sinfulness and commits him or herself fully to God—was necessary for full grace and entry to Heaven. Also, like his mentor, Beecher thought religious revivals—mass conversions, sometimes of entire communities—were the *sine qua non* of a successful minister. Thus, throughout his long career, Lyman Beecher committed himself not only to his own pulpit but also to traveling to revival meetings.

Lyman Beecher "married up" when he wed Roxana Foote (Beecher) in 1799. While his father, David Beecher was very learned and relatively well off, he was a blacksmith by trade; a member of Connecticut's artisanal class. Roxana, on the other hand, was the daughter of a prominent merchant and lawyer in Guilford, Connecticut. The descriptions of her suggest the mutability of the gender conventions of the Early Republic period, when the prescribed roles for white women were transitioning from the "goodwife" of the colonial era to the Republican mother of the early national period. Like her colonial mother and grandmother, Roxana Beecher was skilled at the tasks of housewifery passed down from one generation to the next in preindustrial New England. These skills included spinning wool, mending clothing, planting and tending a garden, and even cutting wood. She was also a talented artist, skilled in embroidery; "an essential accomplishment then."[4] And Roxana's specialty, drawing cameo portraits on ivory, contributed to dozens of family keepsakes.

But Roxana Beecher was also an intellectual, who had as her "constant resource" an encyclopedia that she shared with her sister, Mary Foote, who lived with the Beechers in East Hampton. Roxana Beecher was fluent in French and read voraciously, including complicated mathematical and scientific treatises. She was an assiduous scholar, who worked on and researched a problem until she found a solution. Catharine Beecher recalled her mother and Aunt Mary studying the new science of chemistry together, trying "a great many experiments…. sometimes with the most ludicrous results."[5]

Roxana Beecher's interest in intellectual pursuits was not unusual for the daughter of a Connecticut merchant in the early national period. She grew up during the Revolutionary era, when philosophers, ministers, and political leaders were developing new ideas about the role women should play in the political life of the republic. Women did not emerge from the Revolution in a position of political leadership, of course. Indeed, they experienced little practical change in terms of legal status, remaining subject to their male relatives under feme covert status. Regardless of the status of their families, American women had no right to property, to the vote, or to office holding. But a wedge did appear in terms of women's education. In the new republic, many argued, women had a special role to play as mothers to future (male) citizens. Women needed to be schooled in literature, philosophy, and social and natural sciences in order to inculcate their sons with the proper knowledge and values to become virtuous citizens of the republic. Historians, led by Linda Kerber, call this theory of women's role "Republican Motherhood." By definition, Republican Motherhood applied only to white women. For virtuous citizens, as the nation's founders saw it, could only come from the ranks of white Americans. This ideal influenced women's role and education more in the northern United States than in the South. It is certain to have had influence in the Beecher household.

Ideas thus mattered in the Beecher home. Catharine Beecher recalled long hours at the table, where her parents and her Aunt Mary Foote would engage in philosophical debates and discussion. Lyman Beecher relied on his wife and sisters-in-law for intellectual companionship and feedback "He never was satisfied with his writings till he had read them over to mother and Aunt Mary or Aunt Esther," Beecher recalled and "our house became in reality a school of the highest kind."[6] Certainly for Catharine Beecher, whose career as a reformer of women's education included incorporating the study of hard sciences and mathematics, these formative experiences would prove to be essential.

Almost immediately upon marrying Lyman Beecher, Roxana Beecher was challenged to make a home in rustic East Hampton. In the spring of 1800, the Beechers purchased a two-story shingled house in the Long Island community. They spent $800 for the house, plus an additional $300 in repairs, including fixing the floors, finishing the bedrooms, and building a new fireplace. Roxana declared that, once completed, it would be "quite a convenient house," and she did her best to make it comfortable, even if that meant bucking the tide of her neighbors. For example, the Beechers installed the first carpet in town—one from fibers that Roxana spun and dyed herself, then painted with oil paints that her brother in New York City procured for her. Before this point, "there was not a carpet from end to end of the town."[7] Sanded floors sufficed. Lyman Beecher's parishioners were flummoxed by the rug. The church deacon, upon entering the house for the first time wondered, "D'ye think ye can have all that, *and Heaven too?*"[8] Roxana Beecher's carpet lasted for years, eventually covering the floor of Catharine Beecher's bedroom in Litchfield.

The story of Roxana's rug became legendary in the Beecher family. But it is not just an emblem of her worldliness in contrast to the rustic simplicity of her husband's parishioners. It also illustrates the beginnings of what historian Richard Bushman has identified as the "refinement of America." From the mid-eighteenth century forward, all but the poorest Americans gained access to some kind of consumer goods. These goods came in the form of tea sets, teas and refined sugar, and household furnishings including carpets. Consumer goods came into the reach of a greater swathe of Americans both in urban and rural areas thanks to early mass production of household items. Roxana Beecher's carpet was a novelty in East Hampton but a few years after the Beechers lived there, most of their neighbors would probably have had carpets of their own, along with other mass-produced consumer goods.

While Lyman Beecher's job came with a good deal of local prestige, the life of a minister was not lucrative at that time. Beecher's position in East Hampton was particularly precarious as the parish was poor and could ill afford to pay his salary of $400 per year, plus firewood. By comparison, Lyman Beecher's son, Henry Ward Beecher, would become one of the most famous ministers in nineteenth-century America and drew a salary of $100,000 per year (over $2 million today). Lyman was not so fortunate. He also traveled frequently, leaving his wife alone to manage a financially strapped household and a growing number of children. Roxana's letters from this period reflect a sense of isolation. She lamented that neither her mother nor sister was nearby to help with childcare, and her friends wrote infrequently. For Roxanna, solace came from her children. She wrote to her sister that "Catharine's prattle and the smiles of my little boy contribute to enliven many a gloomy moment."[9] Nevertheless, it was a difficult life marked by hard work.

As their family grew by a child almost each year between 1800 and 1805, the Beechers sought other sources of income. In addition to taking in boarders, Roxana Beecher and Mary Foote opened a school for girls, who also boarded with the Beechers. To their five students, Roxana and Mary taught languages including English and French as well as drawing, painting, and embroidery. In watching her mother run the school, Catharine Beecher was inadvertently being trained for her own career.

Despite her parents' financial concerns, Catharine Beecher remembered the East Hampton home fondly. She recalled frolicking with her siblings in the ocean, scavenging plums and cranberries near the beach, and gathering around her father while he played violin. While his sermons preached fire and brimstone, at home Lyman Beecher was charismatic, warm, and loving, and all of his children described him fondly. Even in in old age, Lyman Beecher's children remembered him as a prankster, always up for a game. Catharine Beecher's sister, Harriet Beecher Stowe, eleven years her junior, declared her father "famous for his power of exciting family enthusiasm."[10] She recalled "a great household inspired by a spirit of cheerfulness and hilarity."[11] For instance, Lyman had a running joke with his sister, Esther, where he would ask her to find his lost hat, although he always well knew where it was. Other times, when the Beecher children were late coming downstairs in the morning, Lyman would stand on the stairs and play a "monstrous tune" on the violin until everyone appeared.[12] Catharine, in particular, remembered Lyman as a playmate, whose jokes included holding her out of a top floor window by her hands or jokingly dunking her head in a wash tub.

By all accounts, Catherine and Lyman Beecher shared a special bond. Harriet Beecher Stowe remembered that Catharine was their father's "favorite and companion, and he was always more than indulgent toward her pranks and jokes."[13] Indeed, while Catharine Beecher has come down in history as dour and didactic, as a child and young woman, she was famous for being funny and fun-loving and she inherited her father's penchant for practical jokes. To Harriet Beecher Stowe, Catharine Beecher's "whole life seemed a constant stream of mirthfulness."[14]

Roxana Beecher was less jocose than her husband and in her children's memory, she took on a mythic, saintly image. Catharine Beecher recalled her mother as "calm and self-possessed" with an "easy and gentle temperament that could never very strictly enforce any rules." One of Harriet Beecher Stowe's few memories of her mother, who died when she was young, involved her walking into her bedroom to discover her children eating a shipment of rare flower bulbs she had received from her brother who was in New York. The children were very excited to tell her that they had eaten an entire bag of onions. Rather than scolding or punishing them, Roxana Beecher lamented the loss of the beautiful flowers that would have bloomed from these bulbs. Discipline in the household thus fell to Lyman, who was as quick to correct his children when they acted out of turn as he was to frolic with them on the beach or in the parlor.

By 1810, Lyman Beecher had finally found it impossible to support his family of seven on his salary in East Hampton and began to cast about for a more lucrative position. The Beechers needed money not just for daily necessities, but also to educate their children, for this was a fundamental priority. Lyman Beecher found a job in Litchfield, Connecticut, a town that Harriet Beecher Stowe described as "half Hebrew theocracy, half ultra-democratic republic."[15] Litchfield claimed about 4,600 residents, most of whom were staunch Christians.

Along with Massachusetts, Vermont, and New Hampshire, Connecticut maintained an established religion after the American Revolution, requiring taxpayers to support the Congregationalist Church. The residents of Litchfield also historically favored the Federalists—the Hamiltonian party that supported internal improvements, strong central government, and reform. When the Beechers moved to Litchfield it looked in some ways the same as it did in 1780: four main streets radiated out from a town green with Reverend Beecher's church at its center. So conservative was the town that even in the 1810s older men could be seen strolling these streets in colonial dress, wearing buckled knee breeches and tri-cornered hats atop powdered wigs as opposed to the trousers and top hats worn by younger men.

Despite these ties to tradition, Litchfield—like many New England towns—was experiencing the upheaval that accompanied the Market Revolution of the early nineteenth-century. Farming had long ceased to be a viable occupation. The sons of Litchfield were seeking their fortunes away from home, in cities like New Haven, Boston, and New York, and the more fertile fields of the west, particularly Ohio, known by some as the "Western Reserve of Connecticut."

But relative to East Hampton, Litchfield was a cosmopolitan town, a center of wealth and education. Litchfield housed Judge Tapping Reeve's Litchfield Law School, the country's first school devoted exclusively to law, boasting such alumni as John C. Calhoun and Rufus King. More importantly for Catharine Beecher, Litchfield was the home of Miss Sarah Pierce's Litchfield Female Academy, one of the nation's preeminent ladies' academies. Miss Pierce was a parishioner of Reverend Beecher and in exchange for his counsel, offered free tuition to his children. Catharine Beecher began her course of study at the age of ten. As a local, she was unusual among her peers at the Female Academy. Most of the students came from communities around New England and boarded with nearby families, including the Beechers, in order to attend the renowned school.

Catharine Beecher thrived academically and socially at Miss Pierce's. She had had no formal schooling before entering the Academy; there were no female academies in East Hampton. So, while her brothers had attended school, Beecher herself studied literature, geography, and mathematics—as well as knitting, embroidery, and painting—at home under her mother's tutelage. Miss Pierce's offered a standard curriculum for ladies, "instructions on those rules of delicacy and propriety so important for every young woman," including "ladylike manners" and "cultivated and refined conversation."[16] This focus was in keeping with a general understanding that, by the early nineteenth-century, the daughters of wealthy Americans were to be relatively leisured. For them, piano playing and etiquette were more important skills than spinning or needlework, for which they would likely rely on servants. Within a few years, Miss Pierce would reform her curriculum under the supervision of her nephew John Brace. Brace would emphasize such academic subjects as history, geography, chemistry, astronomy, and botany. But during Beecher's years at the school, the curriculum focused mainly on reading, writing, arithmetic, drawing, painting, and music. Beecher also remembered that students were encouraged to exercise every day, and Pierce, an avid walker herself, frequently led groups of students on evening strolls through Litchfield. Physical education was not yet a part of school curricula, but Sarah Pierce emphasized the need for women to exercise for health as Beecher would later do when she later founded her own school.

The first five Litchfield years were influential for Catharine Beecher, and she described then as an idyll for her family. Her father enjoyed "a period of more unalloyed happiness than any in his whole life," she recalled.[17] Her mother was healthy and content and her parents' relationship loving and companionate. And the children were "full of health and spirits, under a wise and happy family government."[18]

The Beechers' house was a social as well as moral center in the town of Litchfield. The two-story white house, surrounded by a host of outbuildings such as barn and privy, was full of activity. In addition to the eight Beecher children and their two servants, the family hosted boarders—students at Miss Pierce's or the law school—and entertained nearby neighbors and friends and families passing through Litchfield. Catharine Beecher's beloved Aunt Mary visited frequently, as did many of Roxana Beecher's former pupils from East Hampton who boarded with the Beechers while attending Miss Pierce's school. Beecher's parishioners called frequently, as did ministers visiting from other towns. And each Wednesday evening, the students from the law school came to Beecher's home for a theology recitation. Miss Pierce's students came as well, on Saturdays, for lectures on scripture. The house was rambling but rustic. Children doubled and tripled up in beds, washed up in a kitchen basin, and relieved themselves in the outhouse. Serious study and prayer were required of the Beecher children. Frivolous pursuits such as dancing were forbidden. Christmas and birthdays passed without celebration. Still, looking "back to those days," Catharine Beecher recollected, "an impression of sunshine, love, busy activity, without any memory of a jar or cloud."[19]

But a cloud was indeed on the horizon. In 1816, Roxanna Beecher died of consumption, leaving behind a family of eight children. At 16, Catharine Beecher was the eldest. The youngest, Charles, was only a year old. While Lyman's sister, Esther Beecher, moved in to help with the household and child rearing duties, Catharine Beecher felt compelled, after her mother's death, to drop out of Miss Pierce's and assume the role of surrogate mother to her younger siblings. Never one to embrace domestic pursuits when her mother was alive, upon Roxana's death Catharine took on the responsibilities of housewifery: making clothing for herself and her siblings as well as learning to cook and care for their daily needs. For Catharine, caring for the home and the children may have been her way of grieving her mother. It also likely planted the seeds for her future domestic philosophies. These duties lasted but a year, however, because in 1817, Lyman Beecher returned from an extended visit to Boston engaged to 27-year-old Harriet Porter.

Like her predecessor, Porter came from an established New England family. Her father was a well-respected doctor, her mother was a member of the Maine elite. Harriet's brother Cyrus was a congressman, her brother, Rufus Porter, a member of both the Continental Congress and the Constitutional Convention and later Senator from New York. Harriet Beecher Stowe recalled her first impression of her stepmother:

> She seemed to us so fair, so delicate, so elegant that we were almost afraid to go near her. We must have been rough, red-cheeked, hearty country children, honest, obedient, and bashful. She was peculiarly dainty and neat in all her ways and arrangements; and I remember I used to feel breezy, and rough, and rude in her presence.[20]

By today's standards, Beecher's second marriage might seem to follow too closely the death of his first wife. But a quick remarriage was not uncommon in the early nineteenth-century. By all accounts, Lyman Beecher was grief stricken by the death of Roxana, whom he viewed as his domestic *and* intellectual partner. Harriet Beecher Stowe recalled his despondency at her absence at the first Thanksgiving after Roxanna died:

> When all were in order, and father was to 'ask the blessing,' we waited long in silence, while the great tears stole down his cheeks amid the sighs and tears of all around. Then followed, in a calm, subdued voice, such an

offering of patient, peaceful thankfulness and love, as if the gentle spirit we mourned was near, shedding peace and comfort from her wings.[21]

And Lyman Beecher himself wrote, in a letter to a friend that, while the children were adjusting to the death of their mother, he himself felt "a sensation of loss which nothing alleviates—a solitude which no society interrupts.... I only feel daily, constantly, and with deepening impression, *how much I have had*, for which to be thankful, and how much I have lost."[22]

Nonetheless, romantic notions of marriage and home were just beginning to develop. Lyman Beecher mourned deeply for Roxana, but his grief did not prevent his need to find another wife. A minister with an active pulpit could not also adequately care for eight children, and certainly not within the gender strictures of the early nineteenth-century. Esther Beecher could not stay on with the Beechers indefinitely. Lyman needed a mate to help run his home and oversee his family.

Harriet Porter herself viewed her marriage not from a stance of passion but rather duty to the Church and the Gospel. As a teenager, Harriet had experienced conversion to Christianity, and a life of devotion to the Church followed. In a sense, her marriage was an extension of this commitment. She made this point in a letter she wrote to Catharine between the announcement of her engagement to Lyman and their marriage:

> In my view, a minister of the Gospel .... is to be considered a messenger from the court of Heaven. His happiness is to be regarded, his comfort to be promoted in every possible way. To be an instrument of good to such is also honorable; it is a preferment, I think, far above the distinctions which usually give pre-eminence in this life.[23]

This duty also extended to becoming a stepmother to Roxana Beecher's children.

Luckily for Harriet Porter, the children received their stepmother warmly. Catharine described her as "everything we could wish .... very kind to us all, and appears desirous to do all in her power for our happiness and comfort," gushing, "we already love her dearly." These words may well have been heartfelt. Harriet Porter may have made a good impression on Catharine Beecher upon her arrival, but Porter and Catharine Beecher were very different from one another, and their relationship quickly grew distant. Where Beecher was jovial and even-tempered, Porter was cold, and subject to periods of depression, a condition, incidentally, which she shared with her husband. Within a year of her arrival, Porter was showing signs of melancholy, leading her twelve-year old stepdaughter Mary to write: "Mamma ... don't laugh any more than she used to."[24] Catharine Beecher likewise noted that Harriet "sometimes failed in manifesting pleasure and words of approval at the well doing of subordinates." But of these faults, Catharine Beecher explained that even "the best of women have opportunities for improvement."²⁵ Nonetheless, for the younger children Harriet would become the only mother they ever knew and as she took over the responsibilities of raising them, their biological mother became virtually sanctified in their memory.

Catharine Beecher did not return to school after her father remarried, but instead continued to care for her brothers and sisters alongside her new stepmother. Even without attending school, she managed to maintain an active social life in Litchfield. Her vivacious personality ensured her many friends and suitors, and she enjoyed sleigh rides, ice-skating, walks around the town, parties, and informal socializing with visitors and friends around town.

In the fall of 1819, at the age of 19, Catharine Beecher traveled to Boston and Portland, Maine to visit family, and participate in the cities' lively social scenes. She perfected her piano playing, wrote poetry, and practiced her needlework and other skills that would prepare her to be a fine, middle-class housewife. At twenty-one, endeavoring to contribute to the family finances, Beecher took up a position in New London, teaching these skills to young ladies in a seminary there. She did not, however, intend to follow in the route of Miss Pierce and eschew domestic life in favor of teaching. Her intention was to get married, and she soon was seriously entertaining the attentions of a young scientist/mathematician and philosopher named Alexander Metcalf Fisher. An evangelical Congregationalist and contributor to Lyman Beecher's magazine, *The Christian Spectator*, Fisher asked for an audience with Catharine Beecher after seeing a poem she had published in her father's magazine. Lyman accepted, and Fisher visited Litchfield from New Haven, where he was a professor at Yale.

Initially, Beecher was less impressed with Fisher than he was with her. Fisher was a brilliant thinker with an impressive career trajectory and a reputation for kindness and sobriety. But he struck Beecher as overly staid and insufficiently emotional, a product, she suggested, of his "devoted and exclusive attention to the abstract sciences" which "almost infallibly will deaden the sensibilities of the heart and destroy social habits." To Beecher, it was important to find a mate who was as affectionate as her father and with whom she could form a companionate relationship like her parents shared. She was not so sure that Alexander Fisher fit the bill. All of his brilliance and renown meant little to her, if her marriage were lacking "the thousand kindnesses and little attentions of affections that give comfort to domestic life."

Catharine Beecher did not give in easily to Alexander Fisher. In the fall of 1821, she cut off correspondence with her suitor, much to the chagrin of her father. Lyman Beecher summoned his daughter to Litchfield, where he demanded that she meet with Fisher in person. She did so in December and by the following month, wrote to her friend Louisa announcing: "I am an 'engaged woman.'"²⁶

It is unclear what accounted for Catharine Beecher's change (and change again) of heart. She described it to her friend Louisa Wait as "a long string of misunderstanding," resolved with the realization that their love was stronger than any differences between them. Perhaps she resented the pressure from her father to marry and take up domestic responsibilities. Perhaps her memories of her happy childhood and her reverence for her father set up a difficult bar for any potential suitor to match. Later, perhaps she determined that she would rather be married and living in New Haven than teaching in New London, where she felt lonely and unhappy. Perhaps she simply needed time to get to know Alexander and found him to be both amiable and brilliant. Whatever the reasons, Beecher had decided firmly to marry Alexander Fisher in January of 1822. Shortly after the announcement of their engagement, Fisher left for Europe for a year's time to explore European approaches to teaching philosophy and mathematics; the marriage was to take place upon his return.

But Alexander Fisher never returned from Europe. His ship, the Albion, ran ashore the craggy west coast of Ireland on April 22, 1822, three weeks after its departure from New York, where Fisher issued his final—and, it turns out, very inaccurate—communication: "Everything seemed to promise a quick, safe, and agreeable passage."[27] Fisher appears to have drowned in his cabin when the ship took on water after capsizing and striking the rocky shore. Soon after his death, Beecher traveled to Franklin, Massachusetts to grieve with Fisher's family. In Franklin, she participated in the formal rituals of mourning. These rituals included several ceremonies and eulogies where Fisher's professional accomplishments were recognized; a special ceremony at Yale's commencement, and the erection of a monument in Franklin—co-sponsored by the Fisher family and Yale University—where Beecher contributed a poem for the inscription. While she helped to memorialize Fisher's past, Beecher began to give serious thought to her own future.

First, while in Franklin, Catharine Beecher resolved the religious doubts that had plagued her since she was a teenager. Despite the entreaties of her father and, more recently her brother Edward, she could not give herself over to God in an act of conversion. In the Puritan faith, conversion meant the acceptance of the soul's sinful state followed by personal atonement for all sins. Only then could one fully submit to God. Catharine Beecher was spiritual and devout, but these traits did not suffice for her father. It was not enough to go to Church, to read the Bible, or even to live a devout life. In Lyman Beecher's Calvinistic faith, a conversion experience was necessary for salvation and salvation was necessary to secure a place in Heaven. Lyman wrote despairing letters to his yet-unsaved children, entreating them to receive God before it was too late.

But Catharine Beecher remained intransigent, through her courtship with Fisher, her engagement, and the mourning period of his death. In fact, Fisher's death added to her religious doubts since he himself had died unsaved. In visiting his childhood home, getting to know his family, and reading through his journals, Beecher discovered evidence of Fisher's "blameless and useful life, his unexampled and persevering efforts to do his duty both to God and man."[28] And yet, according to Calvinist doctrine, Fisher would go to Hell because he had failed to experience conversion before his death. Beecher was devastated and told her brother, Edward, that "no sympathy could soothe a grief 'that knows no consolation's name.'"[29] She could not understand how a person that had lived such an exemplary life could be condemned to Hell. This exacerbated her crisis of faith. Her brother Henry Ward Beecher remembered later that Fisher's death had "broken up and destroyed all the religious teachings of her life. The doctrines she had learned did not sustain her."[30] Indeed, after her time in Franklin, Beecher resolved that she would never be saved. "With this wayward, hard, and sinful heart," she wrote to her father, "I have no hope that I shall persevere in seeking religion."[31] She thus dedicated herself to worldly pursuits.

Of course, she was limited in these pursuits by her gender. While early nineteenth-century women worked in taverns, mills, and as domestic labor in the homes of others, the only professional option for middle-class women was teaching. Beecher herself reflected upon these constraints when she wrote to her father that "there seems to be no very extensive sphere of usefulness for a single woman but that which can be found in the limits of a schoolroom."[32] And so, to the schoolroom Beecher pledged herself. But even within those limits, she pledged to find "a more enlarged and comprehensive boundary of exertion."[33] Beecher left Franklin invigorated by her experience tutoring Alexander Fisher's younger sisters in subjects like chemistry, logic, and philosophy. She had studied Fisher's papers and taught herself algebra and geometry. Six years earlier her mother's death had interrupted her schooling, leading Catharine to focus on domestic duties. Now, Fisher's death brought her back to her love of education. She felt ready to carve out a new space in women's education, one more on par with the curriculum that her brothers had experienced.

After making inquiries and recommendations on her behalf in Hartford, Connecticut, Catharine Beecher's father encouraged her that there was a demand for a ladies' academy in that city. He also expressed his expectation that she would not oversee "only a commonplace, middling sort of school," but rather that she would put all of her "talents and strength into it."[34] Otherwise, Lyman concluded, it would not be worth the effort.

Catharine Beecher agreed. In the spring of 1823, she moved to Hartford, Connecticut. Soon after arriving, she opened a small school that would make a very big impact.

Notes

1 Lyman Beecher, *Autobiography, Correspondence, Etc., of Lyman Beecher*, vol. 1, ed. Charles Beecher (London: S. Low, Son, and Marston, 1863), 103, retrieved from https://books.google.com/.
2 L. Beecher, *Autobiography*, 78.
3 L. Beecher, *Autobiography*, 83.
4 L. Beecher, *Autobiography*, 117.

5 Ibid.
6 L. Beecher, *Autobiography*, 125.
7 L. Beecher, *Autobiography*, 102.
8 L. Beecher, *Autobiography*, 103.
9 Jeanne Boydston, Mary Kelly, and Anne Margolis, *The Limits of Sisterhood: The Beecher Sisters on Women's Rights and Women's Sphere* (Chapel Hill: University of North Carolina Press, 1988), 15.
10 Harriet Beecher Stowe, *Life and Letters of Harriet Beecher Stowe*, ed. Annie Fields (Cambridge: Riverside Press, 1897), 34.
11 H.B. Stowe, *Life and Letters*, 42.
12 L. Beecher, *Autobiography*, 145.
13 L. Beecher, *Autobiography*, 474.
14 Ibid.
15 Harriet Beecher Stowe, *Oldtown Folks* (Boston: Fields, Osgood & Co., 1869), 1.
16 Catharine Beecher, *Educational Reminiscences and Suggestions* (New York: J.B. Ford and Company, 1874), 25.
17 L. Beecher, *Autobiography*, 189.
18 Ibid.
19 Ibid.
20 L. Beecher, *Autobiography*, 321.
21 L. Beecher, *Autobiography*, 288.
22 L. Beecher, *Autobiography*, 294.
23 L. Beecher, *Autobiography*, 319.
24 L. Beecher, *Autobiography*, 360.
25 C. Beecher, *Educational Reminiscences*, 25.
26 Kathryn Kish Sklar, *Catharine Beecher: A Study in American Domesticity* (New York: W.W. Norton & Company, 1976), 36.
27 Unknown, "Reminiscences of Alexander Metcalf Fisher, late Professor of Mathematics and Natural Philosophy in Yale College," *New Englander and Yale Review* 1:4 (October 1843), 459.
28 L. Beecher, *Autobiography*, 447.
29 L. Beecher, *Autobiography*, 479.
30 Milton Rugoff, *The Beechers: An American Family in the Nineteenth-Century* (New York: Harper & Row Publishers, 1981), 49.
31 L. Beecher, *Autobiography*, 451.
32 Ibid.
33 L. Beecher, *Autobiography*, 451.
34 L. Beecher, *Autobiography*, 459.

2
BEECHER'S CAREER BEGINS

In the spring of 1823, Catharine Beecher settled herself in Hartford, Connecticut, with a mission: to open a school that would provide a quality education to adolescent girls. By the time she left Hartford eight years later, Beecher had overseen the establishment and expansion of one of the most respected female seminaries in the United States. She also had spearheaded and contributed to education reforms that would take hold across the country in subsequent decades. Beecher's time in Hartford and her experience establishing her school reflect crucial developments in the history of American education and reform in the nineteenth-century.

At its opening, Beecher's school was a modest affair—a room above a harness shop with a student population of seven and no formal curriculum. Within just three years, the student body had increased to 100 and the school moved to larger quarters in a church basement. The quick growth of Beecher's academy illustrates a heightened demand for formal educational institutions in the early republic, especially for women.

Indeed, the establishment of the new nation also saw an increased emphasis on education for both the sons and daughters of the new republic. Following the American Revolution, the United States had just gained its independence from a far-off, centralized monarchy, and was embarking on a rare experiment in self-government. Americans of the revolutionary generation were wary of dependency and believed that power left unchecked would too easily become corrupted. They placed a strong emphasis on the importance of a virtuous, independent citizenry, made up of (white) men who would act (and vote) in the interest of the common good rather than out of selfish motives.

It is for this reason that property was a requirement for voting for the first several decades of the United States' history. These property requirements varied from state to state but most stipulated at least forty pounds worth of real estate for voting rights. The founders believed that owning real estate (in the form of land and slaves) ensured one's own independence, whereas if one depended upon another person for his livelihood, he could be swayed too easily to that man's political leanings. Furthermore, they believed that land ownership implied a stake in one's community that would lead the citizen to try to protect its interests over his own selfish ones. Since most of the founders also believed that African Americans, Native Americans, and women of all races were naturally dependent, these groups were—except for rare instances—denied the right to vote as well.

Many American thinkers believed that formal education was, like land ownership, central to creating a virtuous citizenry. Throughout the eighteenth century the daughters of elite families were literate and often learned basic French, but they were not formally educated. Traditionally, women passed the information needed to care for a family and run a home to one another orally, and so, it was argued, attending school was unnecessary for girls. Following the American Revolution, however, the conversation about education and who should be educated shifted. For instance, Philadelphia physician and statesman Benjamin Rush, author and educator Noah Webster and other early national intellectuals argued for the importance of education in creating not only informed but also patriotic citizens who would support the ideals of their new nation. Webster (who would create the first American English dictionary) saw education as crucial to the national project. Through education, Americans would formalize what distinguished them from the British from whom they had just gained independence. Toward this end, American schools would emphasize American history, American English as a formal written and spoken language, and a distinctive American culture. Public schools, Webster argued, would provide American children with "an inviolable attachment to their own country."[1] This applied to women as well as men for these intellectuals argued that women were not only capable of being educated, but should be educated.

For the most part, these education advocates drew no distinction between women's and men's education, seeing both as equally important to the republican experiment. It is tempting for contemporary students of history to look back at the early republic and assume, since they had no political or economic rights, that women were considered intellectually inferior to men as well. But this presentist view is also over-simplified. Many eighteenth-century thinkers believed that women's intellectual capacities were equal to those of men, even though their "natural" dependency made them unreliable citizens. Without enfranchisement, education would become the key to women's political power in the early republic and some women of the era recognized this. In 1776, future first lady Abigail Adams wrote to her husband John:

> I most sincerely wish that some more liberal plan might be laid and executed for the Benefit of the rising Generation, and that our new constitution

may be distinguished for Learning and Virtue. If we mean to have Heroes, Statesmen, and Philosophers, we should have learned women.[2]

Adams was not alone in her belief that educated women would be important participants in the new republic. Many education advocates argued that women were *morally superior* to men and thus *required* educational opportunities. Among them, essayist Judith Sargent Murray claimed that education would better prepare women for their natural roles as wives and mothers. Murray also saw education as a way for women to gain autonomy, in line with the new country's rhetoric of independence and individualism. This newfound independence would not challenge gender roles, she assured her readers. Instead, educated women would be more willing to embrace the home and their roles in influencing the civic values and morality of their husbands, brothers, and sons. These women would be Republican Mothers.

The argument for women's education was bolstered as well by a redefinition of marriage from an economic arrangement to marriage as a companionship, a shift begun in the late eighteenth century. While financial matches remained important, especially among the children of the wealthy, the idea of marriage for love gained traction over the course of the eighteenth century. Lyman and Roxanna Beecher offered an example—to their daughter Catharine as well as to contemporary readers—of a marriage among intellectual equals, one which early republican thinkers would have held up as an ideal. These same thinkers championed women's education to ensure that women could contribute as much intellectually to their marriages as their husbands. Female education also was important to women's perceived duties as wives and mothers. In order to run proper households, women needed to have certain skills and knowledge that an education could provide them—maintaining household accounts and balancing budgets, managing estates in their husbands' absence, writing letters, and myriad other tasks.

But while education was central to the republican task, the Constitution did not provide for state-sponsored education for either boys or girls. With a few short-lived exceptions, states did not offer funding for formal education, which was the province of local governments and private citizens. In practice, educational opportunities varied by region. American education was so decentralized and informal that the nomenclature is frustratingly imprecise. "Academy" and "seminary" were often used interchangeably, and neither type of school had a formal system of accreditation, a standard curriculum, or any governing body that oversaw the quality or content of the teaching. While higher education—in the form of colleges like Harvard and Yale—was more formalized, elementary, and secondary education was still very much an ad hoc affair.

In rural areas, district schools—funded by the local community—offered the basics of elementary education to local children. In cities, which were located predominantly in the north, private common schools were supported by tuition dollars. These schools were attended largely by the children of middle-income families, such as clerks, artisans, and shopkeepers. The parents of wealthy and upper-class children engaged private tutors in the home—to educate their sons and, in many cases, their daughters as well. This education was supplemented by adventure schools, which might offer lessons in a particular area such as music, Greek and Latin instruction, or dancing.

Poor children did without schooling, or if they were apprenticed, the host family might provide some rudimentary education. They might also receive an education from charity schools run by churches. Among these schools was a series of Free African schools, aimed at educating free Black children in northern cities. These schools, whether rural or urban, offered their pupils a rudimentary education in reading, writing, and arithmetic. Memorization and repetition were the rule of the day.

It is important to note that, in the early nineteenth-century, like today, opportunities were constrained and shaped not only by gender but also by social class and race. Women were not afforded political rights, but neither were African Americans of either gender, nor even property-less White men. Educational opportunities for women depended heavily on social class. Elite and middle-class women had access to formal education; their working-class and poorer counterparts did not. Within these parameters, recent historians have argued, men and women could avail themselves of relatively equal educational opportunities, up to the post-secondary level.

While district and common schools provided an education to younger children, at the turn of the nineteenth-century, there were fewer educational options for older children. But this situation was changing as education became a bit more standardized. In addition, the Enlightenment emphasis on science required that older children learn in more specialized environments than their homes could offer. Furthermore, republican theory held that children should be educated in a community so that social bonds and networks could be formed that would serve them later in their careers. Thus, the rise of the academies: formal institutions that offered complete courses of study to children over the age of 10 or 12. In some cases, the academies had state sanction and a state charter allowing them to operate. But these schools were private in the sense that they received no state aid, relying on tuition for their operations. Tuition varied depending on subject, and by the 1830s and 40s ranged from $3.00 to $12.50 per session (equaling hundreds of dollars in modern currency).

By the turn of the nineteenth-century, there were hundreds of academies in the United States, some male-only, some female-only, and some coeducational. Academy students lived at home or boarded with nearby families (most early republic academies did not offer boarding facilities). While some academies offered a course of study in the classics, they generally offered a more practical education than the more exclusive colleges that provided a classical liberal-arts education and trained young men for the learned professions of law, medicine, and politics. While there were a number of women's academies and seminaries, in the early nineteenth-century, college students were strictly male. No American college admitted women until the 1830s.

The curricula of academies varied but certain subjects were generally covered. English was most important—encompassing reading, writing, spelling, and in some cases oratory and rhetoric. Many academies also offered composition lessons to both boys and girls. Other subjects offered by most academies included arithmetic, geography, and modern and ancient languages and non-academic subjects such as needlework, music, drawing, and dance.

Catharine Beecher intended her Hartford school to follow in the mold of these academies. Like them, it offered a course of study to young women over the age of twelve in English and math, supplemented by sciences, classics, and foreign languages. But early on, Beecher was frustrated by the lack of a system or formal curriculum upon which to base her school. Four years after opening the school, she complained that girls' education was "irregular, superficial, and deficient."[3] Unlike the colleges, which catered to young men, Beecher's school had no library, no textbooks, and very little equipment with which to teach— "no globe or large maps, and most of the time, no blackboard," Beecher recalled years later.[4] Moreover, she had no administrators, so she was tasked not only with teaching, but also with running the school and determining the curriculum. Thus, Beecher remembered, "I had all the responsibilities which in colleges are divided among the faculty, treasurer, and boarding-housekeeper, and at the same time taught four and five hours a day."[5]

As a school administrator and a teacher, Beecher was learning on the fly. No formal institutions of higher education existed for women in the early nineteenth-century (and no teacher training academies until Beecher herself established one) so Beecher essentially had to train herself as well as her teachers. She would take lessons from her brother Edward in Latin, geography, and other advanced subjects in the mornings and then in the afternoons teach the same subject to her students. With only two teachers, Beecher recruited her strongest pupils—including her sister Harriet—to act as assistant teachers. They held study groups in which they would read classical texts like Virgil, Cicero, and Ovid before sharing them with the students.

In her school's early years, Beecher followed a pedagogical model that had existed since the eighteenth century: students would regurgitate the lessons and texts. Teachers did not know "how much was clearly understood, or how much was mere memorizing of words."[6] These recitations—where students stood in front of the teacher and "recited" the lessons back to them—were standard practice in the academies of the early republic, and Beecher was simply replicating her own school experiences. But she was not satisfied with this method of learning or its efficacy and, on a more practical level, she noted that very little learning could occur in the cacophonous atmosphere of one large basement room with multiple recitations occurring at the same time. Beecher recalled the atmosphere as one of "confusion, haste, and imperfection."[7] In addition, she felt compelled to teach a wide range of subjects and her students entered at age twelve with an equally wide range of previous skills and knowledge. Beecher thus oversaw—and her two teachers led—eight classes a day. Not only was this situation exhausting to Beecher and her staff, but it resulted in a superficial education for their students—much breadth but very little depth.

It was clear to Catharine Beecher that a change was in order. In 1826, feeling herself and her school sufficiently settled in Hartford, she set about making the necessary reforms. In so doing, she put in place a new system of education that, along with the schools of Mary Lyons and Emma Willard, would set the template for female education in the early republic and antebellum eras.

In order to establish her school on more solid footing, Beecher began a fundraising appeal to Hartford's elite. The men of Hartford looked askance at the price tag for Beecher's ambitious proposal for a dedicated schoolhouse, complete with six recitation rooms, a lecture hall, a gymnasium (or, as she called it, a calisthenics room), and a study hall that could accommodate 150 students, Beecher turned therefore to their wives. The elite women of Hartford prevailed upon their husbands to fund the Hartford Female Seminary and Beecher learned an important lesson about achieving her goals for reform. As she later recalled: "This was my first experience of the moral power and good judgment of American women, which has been my chief reliance ever since."[8] By early 1827, Catharine Beecher had managed to raise over $5,000 for her school which was incorporated under the formal name of Hartford Female Seminary. She wrote to her brother Edward describing her business plan, "I am not going into *partnership* with anyone," she declared, "I shall be head [of the Hartford Female Seminary] and pay salaries and I *mean to make money by it.*"[9] The jovial Catharine that the Beecher siblings had known in their youth had become a shrewd businesswoman. Beecher's seminary was a formal institution, with an established endowment, and a considered curriculum.

The structure and formality distinguished the Hartford Seminary from other academies of the era, including both Miss Pierce's and Beecher's own school in its very early years. Beecher's choice of the term "seminary" over "academy" reflects her own consideration of this difference. The proposed structure of Beecher's school was like that of the Troy Seminary, which educator Emma Willard opened in Troy, New York in 1821. The Troy Seminary was funded, at Willard's insistence, by a board made up of prominent local men along the lines of male seminaries. Beecher established a similar board and funding structure as she sought to turn her academy into a formal seminary. The reforms Beecher enacted in terms of curriculum, pedagogy, and administration would change the thrust of women's education in the late nineteenth-century and beyond and pave the way for female higher education.

Pedagogically, Beecher's most important contribution was to abandon the rote memorization that characterized American education at that time in favor of hands-on instruction and visual aids such as maps, globes, blackboards, and student drawings. Beecher rightly complained that the recitation system favored "*committing to memory words*, instead of acquiring *ideas*."[10] Instead, she promoted teaching methods that would emphasize critical analysis and lead students to understand not only the facts but the meaning behind them. For example, students were not only asked to learn multiplication tables but to understand the underlying way that the numbers work. In geography, students did not just memorize maps; they created and analyzed them, tasks that required a mastery of longitude and latitude and scale as well as an ability to critically examine spatial relationships. In grammar, they did not merely parse sentences, but rather learned the way that language was constructed.

Beecher enacted rigorous standards of instruction and assessment. Hartford Seminary students learned the basic branches of reading, writing, and math but also geography, chemistry, philosophy, Latin, and Greek. Students had to pass exams in order to move forward in the curriculum. Beecher emphasized division of labor in the classroom, with different, trained instructors in charge of different subjects and small classes with students grouped by ability. This reform reflected Beecher's concern about teacher training. Most academies expected teachers to offer several subjects and to teach groups of students of vastly different skills and levels. Beecher rejected this standard, arguing instead that teachers should specialize in particular subjects and students be tracked according to skills and aptitude, just as they were in men's colleges.

Another important innovation that Beecher proposed was to place moral education on the same level as academic development. Beecher went so far as to argue that moral training—"the correction of the disposition, the regulation of the social feelings, the formation of the conscience, and the direction of the moral character and habits"—was more important than intellectual instruction as an object of education. Teachers and schools, argued Beecher, should be responsible not only for teaching reading, math, and science but also comportment, manners, decorum, modesty, even personal hygiene and neatness in dress. According to Beecher, the body and mind should both be strengthened through education. She even hired a calisthenics instructor to teach what today would be called a physical education course, although this term would not be used for several decades.

This branch of her educational philosophy provided the foundation for Beecher's argument that teaching, as a profession, should be reserved to women. "It is to *mothers*, and to *teachers*, that the world is to look for the character which is to be enstamped on each succeeding generation, for it is to them that the great business of education is almost exclusively committed," Beecher wrote to the to the Trustees of the Hartford Female Seminary. "What is *the Profession of a Woman?*" she continued.

> Is it not to form immortal minds, and to watch, to nurse, and to rear the bodily system, so fearfully and wonderfully made, and upon the order and regulation of which, the health and well-being of the mind so greatly depends?[11]

Women would come to dominate the teaching profession in the nineteenth-century and even at this early point, the teachers at Beecher's school were female. But throughout the nation, men formed a majority of teachers. Tutors who educated the children of the wealthy were usually young men, often college students. And private academies employed male teachers as often as female. Miss Pierce's school, for example, was run by Miss Pierce's nephew, John Brace.

Beecher argued that women were naturally more affectionate, sympathetic, and moral. These traits made them better suited to train children both in academic and non-academic subjects. Indeed, this enhanced morality gave women not only a right but a duty to serve as the nation's teachers; they offered a hedge against "the inroads of vice, infidelity, and error," that would otherwise overtake the nation. "Let the leading females of this country become pious, refined and active and the salt is scattered through the land to purify and save," Beecher declared.[12] These arguments reflected the long-term influence of Republican Motherhood.

As part of her educational vision, Beecher sought to add an administrator who would be in charge of moral development. She also argued for boarding facilities at the school. These facilities would ensure that the teachers and administrators could live among the students and thus influence their moral development even outside of the classroom. These plans for moral education would not bear fruit in Beecher's school. Most of her funders held the mainstream view that moral education was the responsibility of churches, not of schools. Beecher thus raised enough money for equipment and facilities but could not sway Hartford's elite to fund either a new administrator or a residency hall. But Catharine Beecher's thinking on moral education formed the basis for her later ideas and proposals about women's moral duties and prerogatives both as mothers and as teachers.

In the antebellum era, Beecher's claims of women's natural moral superiority and ability to nurture would coincide with a vastly increased demand for teachers as a result of the establishment of the common school system. Thus, Beecher would pave the way for women to dominate the teaching profession. Hartford Seminary would serve not just as a finishing school for women, or an institution devoted to preparing women to run proper middle-class households but in fact, as a formal training ground for teachers. Its students would go on to teaching careers around the country, many of them establishing their own schools both for primary and teacher education.

Catharine Beecher went a long way toward implementing the educational reforms she proposed in Hartford. By 1830, the school was running as a full women's seminary. It had over 100 students and eight teachers, a permanent location, a rigorous curriculum, an endowment of over $5,000, and a national reputation. It would continue to provide a quality women's education for sixty years. Beecher had made a name for herself in Connecticut and beyond as an educational pioneer. She had established herself as a member of Hartford's elite and enjoyed an active social life.

At the same time, Catharine Beecher was tired. She confessed to her brother Edward her fear:

> I am so much engaged in moulding *(sic)*, correcting, and inspecting the character of *others* that I sometimes fear my own will be a 'cast away,' but then I comfort myself with the reflection that 'he that watereth, shall himself be watered,' and I cannot say but the promise has in a measure been verified to me.[13]

Despite comforting herself that she was promoting the greater good, Beecher's exertions over the past seven years on behalf of her school had exhausted her and to her great disappointment, some of her efforts. She expected that the moral training her students received would result in their having social influence beyond the walls of the Hartford Female Seminary. In turn, Beecher aspired to become a leading moral instructor, replacing the male clergyman who typically oversaw female education. Beecher's goal, however, would not be realized. In Beecher's view these goals could better be achieved with the endorsement of a well-respected female educator, which she hoped would lead to additional donor funding. She had her eye on Zilpah Grant, the associate principle at Mary Lyon's Ipswitch Female Seminary, and offered her a position at Hartford. Grant, however, was critical of the emphasis on decorum—as opposed to spiritual teachings—at Beecher's school, and turned down the job. Beecher was devastated, likely because she feared that without Grant's support the financial stability of the Harford School was in jeopardy. Failure seemed to be a probability as many community members openly criticized the Harford Seminary for overeducating women, they believed, to the point of being unmarriageable. This must have felt like a personal insult to Beecher, who had consciously made the decision not to marry. She was further despondent when she failed to raise enough money to pay for additional administrators and to establish boarding facilities at her school. In early 1830, Beecher suffered the first major in a series of nervous collapses which would plague her throughout her life. She moved to Boston for a brief period to be with her father, leaving the school under her sister Harriet's direction. Beecher returned to resume the leadership of the Hartford Seminary but by September 1831, she would leave the school permanently. This would begin a cycle that repeated throughout Beecher's life. When faced with failure or rejection she would become ill and retreat from public life. Her projects would fall into the care of a colleague. And when an opportunity arose elsewhere, she embraced it.

In this case, it was an opportunity for her father that drew Beecher from Hartford. Lyman Beecher left his position as head of Boston's Hanover Street Church to accept an invitation to serve as president of the Lane Theological Seminary in Cincinnati. Lyman hoped his children would join him in Ohio and

Catharine was the first to do so. In the spring of 1832 she and her father set out for Cincinnati, "the London of the West." Thus, began a new chapter in their family's history as well as Catharine Beecher's career.

Notes

1 As quoted in Carl F. Kaestle, *Pillars of the Republic* (New York: Hill and Wang, 1983), 7.
2 Abigail Adams to John Adams, 14 August 1776. *Founders Online*, National Archives https://founders.archives.gov/documents/Adams/04-02-02-0058. Original source: *The Adams Papers*, Adams Family Correspondence, vol. 2, *June 1776–March 1778*, ed. L. H. Butterfield (Cambridge, MA: Harvard University Press, 1963), 93–95.
3 Milton Allan Rugoff, *The Beechers: An American Family in the Nineteenth-Century* (New York: Harper & Row, 1981), 54.
4 Catharine E. Beecher, *Educational Reminiscences and Suggestions* (New York: J.B. Ford and Company, 1874), 30.
5 C. Beecher, *Educational Reminiscences*, 61.
6 C. Beecher, *Educational Reminiscences*, 31.
7 Ibid.
8 Kathryn Kish Sklar, *Catharine Beecher: A Study in American Domesticity* (New York: W.W. Norton & Company, 1976), 33
9 CEB to Edward Beecher, March 3, 1827, in Jeanne Boydston, Mary Kelly, and Anne Margolis, *The Limits of Sisterhood: The Beecher Sisters on Women's Rights and Women's Sphere* (Chapel Hill: University of North Carolina Press, 1988), 41.
10 Sklar, 13.
11 Catharine Beecher, *Suggestions Respecting Improvements in Education, Presented to the Trustees of the Hartford Female Seminary* (Hartford: Packard and Butler, 1829), 7.
12 Rugoff, 61.
13 CED to Edward Beecher, March 3, 1827, in *The Limits of Sisterhood*, 41-42.

3
OUT WEST

In the spring of 1832, Catharine and Lyman Beecher traveled for several weeks by overland stagecoach from Connecticut to Wheeling, West Virginia. In Wheeling, they boarded a steamboat, which they deboarded three days later in Cincinnati—the "Queen City of the West." This opened an extended—and challenging—period of time in the West for the Beechers. Circumstances—and their own actions and attitudes—placed the Beechers unexpectedly and unwittingly at the center of a series of controversies. These events and their aftermath would make them (especially Catharine Beecher) virtual pariahs in the elite society that at first welcomed them enthusiastically. This isolation would test Beecher sorely. But it also offered a foundation for her to fully develop her theories on women's education and role in American society.

Today Ohio is an anchor of the Midwest. But in the early national period, it was the far west, "unsettled" territory that white settlers viewed as ripe for the picking once the United States established hegemony over the area. During the colonial period, the Leni Lenape Indians had some protection from the British government against encroachment by land-greedy European settlers. This protection stemmed from economic self-interest rather than cultural respect. Great Britain had no interest in committing money or troops to opening these lands to White settlement. But when the Treaty of Paris ended the American Revolution, the British abandoned any oversight of western lands. In 1797, the US Congress organized the Northwest Territory with an eye to eventually incorporating it into the United States. This 260,000 square-mile parcel of land encompassed the states that would become Ohio, Michigan, Indiana, Illinois, Wisconsin, and part of Minnesota. White settlement proceeded rapidly. In 1790, 5 percent of Americans lived west of the Appalachian Mountains. By 1820, that figure had increased to 25 percent.

DOI: 10.4324/b23305-4

By 1803, enough settlers had arrived that Ohio's population exceeded 60,000, making it eligible for statehood. Settlers continued to pour in, arriving first by stagecoach, then by canal and steamboat. Southern farmers moved northward and set down roots in rural areas in the Ohio Valley, creating a southern-influenced culture in these regions. Migrants from New York and New England traveled overland and established towns on the New England model, some of which grew into major cities. These settlements replicated New England institutions such as the Congregationalist and Presbyterian Churches and established Northeast-inspired educational outposts such as Miami University of Ohio, and Lane Seminary. In general, the northern part of Ohio drew more New Englanders. Connecticut claimed land in the "Western Reserve" in the northeastern part of the state and migrants from Connecticut started to settle on those lands as early as the 1790s. After the Erie Canal opened in 1825, it offered an obvious route from New York and New England to the west, and these travelers generally settled in the northern part of Ohio. But though it was located in the South, Cincinnati became a New England pocket, "a Middle States enclave in an upland South environment," according to geographer Donald Meinig.[1]

The Beechers disembarked in a vibrant, bustling city of almost 25,000, shaped by its location on the Ohio River. Trade centered on the waterfront and Cincinnati quickly became a center of steamboat construction and repair. Steamboats plied the river and crowded along its banks, contributing to the sense of bustle and activity. Settlement clustered on the northern bank of the river and ferry boats served to connect the city to its suburbs on the southern, Kentucky banks. Along with the river, the hills to the North served as natural boundaries for the city and also gave it a picturesque setting.

Cincinnati offered much that was familiar to the Beechers. Many friends had relocated there from the East Coast, including several from Litchfield and Hartford as well as their host Samuel Foote, who was Catharine Beecher's maternal uncle. The wealthy Foote was a civic leader in Cincinnati along with Edward King, the son of New York Senator Rufus King and Connecticut-born Nathaniel Wright, who served as the president of the board of trustees at Lane Seminary. Reflecting on the familiarity of Cincinnati society, Beecher observed that "everybody I used to know is here or coming here."[2] She described her potential neighbors approvingly as "New England sort of folks," and the Queen City itself as "A New England city in all its habits."[3]

Cultural opportunities were replete in Cincinnati as well. The western city housed institutions of comfort and entertainment both for travelers and residents, including hotels, restaurants, theaters, bookstores, museums, several grog-shops (early saloons), and an athenaeum where lectures on various topics took place. The city's publishers produced a dozen newspapers and a ladies' magazine. Among its prominent public works and institutions were a water system and reservoir, a hospital, a bank, a "lunatic asylum," and several schools. The elite social scene that Beecher hoped to enter was active and vibrant, sponsoring literary societies such as the Semi-Colon Club (of which Catharine Beecher was a member), and supporting hospitals, schools, and churches such as Lyman Beecher's Second Presbyterian Church. Visiting from Sweden in the 1830s, Karl Arfwedsen marveled at the Queen City's stolidity even in the context of its rapid growth: "Handsome brick houses, wide streets, and magnificent public buildings, strike the astonished eye of the stranger, who expected to find only wooden houses and narrow lanes." Arfwedsen found this situation especially impressive since, as he described it, "a quarter of a century ago, nothing but the primitive forest was standing untouched."[4]

Cincinnati also served as an important distribution point for foodstuffs from the rural hinterlands, which were sold in the city's public markets and distributed overland to Pittsburgh and down the Ohio and Mississippi Rivers as far afield as New Orleans, a major market. Pork processing was a particularly vital industry—over 150,000 hogs were slaughtered there each year in the early 1830s, lending the Queen City a second nickname—"Porkopolis." Cincinnati industry was bustling in other areas as well, including over sixty iron foundries, several flour mills, factories that produced industrial goods such as glass, cotton gins, and barrels for whiskey and flour. The pace of trade increased with the opening of the local Miami Canal and the extension of the Erie Canal that connected it to the Ohio River. These waterways also enhanced communications and the dissemination of information, bringing the once-distant city into a national network of communications. Between the American Revolution and the Civil War new industrial technologies changed the United States from a largely agricultural nation to a commercial economy. National transportation networks were established as the result of steamboats and railroads and infrastructure such as paved roads and canals linked eastern cities with western towns.

Catharine and Lyman Beecher were favorably impressed with the city and its social scene. After her "painful termination" with the Harford Female Seminary Catharine must have had high hopes for the opportunities available to her in Cincinnati.[5] She wrote her sister Harriet "I never saw a place so capable of being rendered a paradise by the improvements of taste as the environs of this city."[6] To Catharine Beecher's delight, the architecture of Cincinnati reminded her of a much older city and many of the residents were also New England transplants. After a month of immersion, Lyman and Catharine Beecher decided to move to Cincinnati. By November, they were settled in, occupying a rented house while they waited six months for their home to be built in the suburb of Walnut Hills. There, they were joined by many of their relations; indeed, the move to Cincinnati involved establishing a veritable Beecher annex in the west, including three of Catharine's adult siblings, Lyman's wife Harriet and their three young children (aged between four and ten).

Not long after settling in Cincinnati, Catharine Beecher made plans to establish a school in the city. It would be, she wrote of "first-rate order [and] ... a model to the West."⁷ Cincinnati was ripe for a women's seminary and its elite were eager to establish one. For Beecher, the school would provide an opportunity to spread her educational reforms and emphasis on training female teachers beyond the East Coast and to the burgeoning west. She lured her Hartford assistant, Mary Dutton to Cincinnati to serve as the school's principal. A week after Dutton's arrival in April 1833, Beecher announced that she would be opening a school under the name of the Western Female Institute.

Unlike the Hartford Seminary, Catharine Beecher took a hands-off approach to the Western Female Institute. She loaned her name and reputation to the school and oversaw fundraising. Her sister, Harriet Beecher Stowe, served as co-principal. But Mary Dutton managed the daily administration of the school. Beecher did not teach, aside from delivering guest lectures from time to time. Instead, she wrote essays and traveled the country delivering lectures offering her proposals for women's education.

These proposals were rooted in the vast demographic changes occurring in the United States at the time, particularly immigration and the expansion of the white, male electorate. While immigrants were arriving in the United States from the early colonial period onward, their numbers increased significantly in the 1830s after a lull following the Revolution.

In 1820, just over 8,000 immigrants entered the United States, and in 1830, 98.5% of Americans were native-born. But between 1831 and 1840, these numbers ballooned—almost 600,000 immigrants came into the country, mainly from Ireland, Germany, and Britain. Another 1.7 million immigrants flooded American shores in the 1840s. Most of the immigrants who settled in Cincinnati hailed from Germany. The city's German population rose from 5 percent of the total to 30 percent in the 1830s and then doubled in the 1840s. As they did in other American cities, German Cincinnatians created an important ethnic enclave. Known as "Over-the-Rhine," Cincinnati's Little Germany remained an important center of German heritage and culture throughout the nineteenth-century and into the 1900s.

While the nation was growing larger and more demographically diverse in the antebellum era, important changes occurred in the realm of politics as the eligible electorate expanded. Suffrage was a state right, not a federal one and individual states determined requirements for voting. During the period between the Revolution and the Civil War, all states gradually abandoned property requirements for voting. By 1850, most adult White men were able to vote.

The expansion of male suffrage was rhetorically in line with the promise of "life, liberty, and the pursuit of happiness" made in the Declaration of Independence. Citizenship too was easier to obtain than it would be during the twentieth and twenty-first centuries. Immigrants were required to reside in the United States for five years and renounce allegiance to their home country. For some native-born Americans, however, the ease in which immigrants were able to integrate into the United States was threatening. For example, during the 1850s the Know-Nothing Party claimed that Catholic immigrants were a threat to the stability of the nation because they would be more loyal to the Pope than the President of the United States. But this faction of nativists were not the only ones that feared Catholic influence. Lyman Beecher also saw Catholic immigrants as a threat. In his book, *A Plea for the West*, Beecher warned that the United States was vulnerable to a "corrupting influence."[8] Other groups, however, used this influx of immigrants to gain political majority.

In the nation's growing cities, burgeoning political machines dominated local politics and recognized the potential of the immigrant vote. Political organizations like New York's Tammany Hall offered favors, jobs, and money to immigrant voters in exchange for a guarantee that they would turn out for Tammany in local elections. This symbiotic relationship between immigrant voters and political machines helped the latter to maintain power and dominate urban politics well into the twentieth century. At the same time and for the same reasons, this relationship also rankled middle-class and elite voters, reformers, and politicians. They despised the corruption of the political machines but just as much, they resented the growing influence and power of immigrant and working-class voters.

While white men battled for political authority, others remained disenfranchised. Simultaneous to state legislatures expanding suffrage for white men, they excluded Black men and women of all races. Native Americans were also denied suffrage, an ironic exclusion given that many states allowed voting rights to newly arrived immigrants. This policy especially occurred in Western states; eager to draw settlers so they could expedite the process of statehood. Western territories offered voting rights as an incentive for immigrants to settle there; the same incentive would be offered to women, who gained suffrage first in the western states and later nationally. Also, as the movement for women's suffrage gained steam in the late 1840s, many of its advocates argued that white, middle-class and elite women were certainly more deserving and would be more judicious in the use of the vote than those they deemed to be their social inferiors—working-class, poor, and immigrant men.

Catharine Beecher was no suffragist, and she shared the concern of her father and others that these "ignorant native and foreign adults are now voters, and have a share in the government of the nation."[9] Unlike the suffragists, Beecher did not extend this argument into a demand for the vote for educated women. She argued, however, that education could ameliorate the problem, and she certainly saw a role for women as educators.

In 1835, she expounded on these ideas, which she published as *An Essay on the Education of Female Teachers, for the United States*. Like many of her contemporaries, Beecher responded to the rapid changes in American society and culture with alarm. In the communities of the east, she argued, "the education of the lower classes is deteriorating, as it respects moral and religious restraints."[10] To make matters worse for Beecher, "at the same time thousands and thousands of degraded foreigners, and their ignorant families, are pouring into this nation at every avenue."[11] Left unchecked, she feared that the nation would be left "in the hands of ignorance and vice."[12]

Her condescension toward immigrants did not extend to a call to ban them, as might occur today. Rather, Beecher argued, they needed to be assimilated to (Anglo-Protestant) American society and culture through education. Here, Beecher offered her pedagogical prescriptions for America's problems as well as advocating women as the nation's primary educators. To properly educate the rapidly growing population of the country, Beecher argued that the corps of trained teachers needed to be expanded by 90,000. These ranks should be made up primarily by women, Beecher held, since they were by nature maternal and morally superior to men. Thus, women were naturally suited to the task of imparting moral values to youngsters.

Furthermore, Beecher claimed (in a note that contemporary teachers will appreciate), that the low pay made the job of teaching more appropriate for women than for men. While men were far more inclined to seek more lucrative careers, she argued, women would settle for the meager salary that teaching afforded. Rather than advocating an increase in pay or more respect for the important profession of teaching, Beecher suggested that women would be willing to work for the "scanty pittance" a teacher's paycheck offered.[13] For training, Beecher called for a national system of women's seminaries to prepare women for the teaching profession. The Western Female Institute was to serve as a model.

But in order to get that model up and running, Beecher needed money. As she had done in Hartford, she sought funding from the Cincinnati elite whose circles she had spent time infiltrating. Her initial popularity with these wealthy families likely emboldened her fundraising efforts. But while at first Beecher had been well-received in Cincinnati, once she began to seek support for her education plans, she began to lose favor among her friends and neighbors.

To some extent, Beecher's fall from grace in Cincinnati was out of her control. A fierce conflict over abolition—the movement to abolish slavery—ripped through Lane Seminary and its leader—Lyman Beecher—was implicated in the controversy. In the 1830s, abolition was becoming a formal movement, with adherents across the North. In 1831, editor and abolitionist William Lloyd Garrison founded *The Liberator*, an antislavery newspaper that would become an influential voice in the movement for abolition. The movement continued to gain formal steam with the first Antislavery Convention, held in Philadelphia in 1833.

While few Americans—North or South—would describe themselves as abolitionists, the movement was vocal enough that proslavery forces began to see it as a threat. Violence broke on both sides of the cause. In 1831 an enslaved Virginian, Nat Turner, led an armed revolt that result in the deaths of approximately sixty whites. In retaliation, local soldiers, militia men, and vigilantes brutally killed more than 100 African Americans, many of whom were innocent. Nat Turner, himself, would be hung, and his followers either captured or killed. The Nat Turner Rebellion reflected a demand for abolition among Virginia's slave population. For slaveholders, who imagined their slaves incapable of planning rebellions on their own, the insurrection insighted terror. The Virginia Legislature debated abolishing slavery out fear of future rebellions but instead enacted laws to further restrict the activities of free and enslaved African Americans, including the banning gatherings of more than five people, stricter literacy laws, and harsh punishments for owning a firearm or inciting violence against a White person. Other southern states followed suit. For southern slaveholders, the Nat Turner Rebellion also seemed to indicate that the abolitionists were moving beyond talk into action, rousing their slaves to demand their freedom at gunpoint.

Yet anti-abolition sentiment was by no means limited to the slaveholding South. In 1834 and 1835, anti-abolition riots occurred in New York, Philadelphia, and other northeastern cities. Anti-abolition forces in these cities feared the disruption that abolitionists posed to the established order. Not only did these antislavery advocates demand an immediate abolition of slavery but some also championed racial equality and integration, a step too far for most White Americans. Many White laborers also opposed abolition out of the fear that a mass of newly freed slaves would move to northern cities and pose competition to them in an already extremely tight and exploitative job market. This position was ironic given that many of these White, urban laborers were in fact recent immigrants who took over the menial job sectors that African Americans had dominated for years. On several occasions in the mid-1830s, the anger and fear of anti-abolitionists came to a head in the form of riots and individual acts of violence against abolitionist targets, Black churches and businesses, as well as prominent abolitionists.

Even in its early days, Cincinnati had a significant Black population. Between 1788 and 1829, countless African Americans from the slave state of Kentucky—some born free, some former slaves who had gained their freedom, some escaped fugitives who had claimed their freedom by escaping to the free territory across the river—moved into Ohio. Ohio's Black population swelled to 9,568 by 1830, over 1,000 of whom lived in Cincinnati. During that year, the Black population of Cincinnati also increased by more than 1,000 people; twenty years earlier in 1810, only eighty-two African Americans had moved to Cincinnati. Now, the community was growing rapidly and establishing churches, homes and businesses in the predominantly Black neighborhood of Bucktown.

The presence of the African American inhabitants did not, however, create acceptance among white residents and an uneasy tension existed between Black and White Cincinnati. In an effort to distinguish themselves socially in an increasingly diverse and competitive urban environment, Irish immigrants, relegated to the bottom of the social hierarchy, found advantages in positioning their own whiteness against African Americans, many of whom had lived in Cincinnati longer than them. Competition over jobs exacerbated these divisions and individual acts of violence and discrimination against African Americans were common. Members of Cincinnati's White elite also bristled at the influx of African Americans, reacting out of a sense of White supremacy and class privilege as well as a sense of solidarity with white slaveholders across the Ohio River. Discriminatory "Black codes" limited Black Ohioans' mobility, and denied them the right to testify in court, to sue Whites, or to attend public schools. These racist tendencies blurred with opposition to abolition. A very small percentage of Americans supported abolition at that point but even those individuals who opposed slavery tended, like the Beechers, to support more gradualist and conciliatory approaches to ending slavery, such as colonization schemes. Cincinnati's business leaders also feared alienating slaveholding Whites, some of whom who lived just a few miles away and with whom they were economically interdependent.

In 1829 Bucktown was a target of white racist mobs. Faced with property damage and physical threats, over 1,000 African Americans fled Cincinnati for other parts of Ohio and even Canada. Those who stayed in Cincinnati braved mob violence and inequality; many were young and without the financial means to start over in a new city. It was easier for an African American to secure a job in Cincinnati than in smaller towns. Others remained in Cincinnati because of its proximity to enslaved family members in the South. As many as two-thirds of the African American population were working to purchase a loved one from slavery. Bolstered by the African Methodist Episcopal Church, the Black community of Cincinnati set about rebuilding.

Violence erupted again, however, in the summer of 1836 when anti-abolitionist rioters destroyed James G. Birney's weekly abolitionist newspaper, *The Philanthropist*. Birney, who had grown up in a slaveholding family, embraced first the cause of colonization and more recently began to demand full abolition, including in the pages of *The Philanthropist*, which he published in New Richmond, Ohio, about twenty miles away from Cincinnati, and distributed not only in Ohio but also in slaveholding Kentucky. The growing chorus of anti-abolitionist voices in Cincinnati began to amass against Birney and his press. In January of 1836, a group of anti-abolitionists—including some of Cincinnati's most prominent leaders—gathered at a meeting to demand the end to abolitionist publications in Ohio. Over the first half of the year, petitioners demanded that the government shut down Birney's paper and, failing in that endeavor, they began to threaten Birney himself. In April, they unsuccessfully attacked Birney's press, prompting the Ohio Antislavery Society to take over its administration and to move the press to Cincinnati.

But the antislavery forces were hardly mollified. In July, a mob broke into Birney's office and again tried to destroy his printing press. Birney, undeterred, continued to publish his paper. Cincinnati's anti-abolitionists responded by attacking Birney's office and destroying his printing press. Other abolitionists and African Americans were also targeted in the city. It took days and a declaration of martial law to end the riot, and in the end, several Blacks were dead, and more were forced to flee when their homes were burned.

The damage to race relations in Cincinnati was equally considerable. Battle lines were drawn between abolitionists on one hand and anti-abolitionists on the other. Among the ranks of the latter were individuals who opposed slavery but were more inclined to support colonization and to sympathize with slaveholders than they were to align themselves with radical abolitionists. Indeed, the mob in Cincinnati reflected a diverse group of people. Among those who attacked Birney's press were some of the city's most prominent men.

The Beecher family took different stances on the violence in Cincinnati. All were opposed to slavery, but Lyman and Catharine Beecher remained cautious in their opposition. For other of the Beecher children, however, abolition was becoming a hard issue to ignore. The first Beecher to radically oppose slavery was Catharine's brother George, who joined the Antislavery Society in 1836. The following year he convinced their brother William to join as well. Another brother, Edward, adopted abolition in 1837, after his friend the antislavery journalist Elijah Lovejoy was shot during an anti-abolitionist riot. For the most famous abolitionist Beechers, however, the 1836 riot was a catalyst for their radicalism. In a letter to her husband, Calvin Stowe, Harriet, already a budding abolitionist, described the riots in Cincinnati. "For my part, I can easily see how such proceedings may make converts to abolitionism, for already my sympathies are strongly enlisted for Mr. Birney, and I hope that he will stand his ground and assert his rights," Harriet declared.[14] Henry, who had previously remained moderate on the issue to appease his father, was emboldened by the violence to speak his mind. He wrote an editorial condemning mob violence and later, when the violence once again escalated, volunteered to join a posse designated to patrol the streets. Harriet was horrified one day to find Henry making bullets in anticipation of his lookout. She wrote to Calvin,

> For a day or two we did not know but there would actually be war to the knife, as was threatened by the mob, and we really saw Henry depart with pistols with daily alarm, only we were too full of patriotism not to have sent every bother we had, rather than not have had the principles of freedom and order defended.[15]

Cincinnati was a hotbed of racial strife, and the Beecher family was at its epicenter, even those members who did not want to be.

In the winter of 1834, anti-abolitionist conflicts took center stage at Lyman Beecher's Lane Seminary. Beecher himself was not proslavery, but he was not an abolitionist. Like his daughter Catharine, Lyman Beecher supported the more conservative—and far more widespread—colonization movement. Colonization gained many prominent adherents in the 1830s and 1840s including James

Madison and Secretary of State Henry Clay and it received the support of several state legislatures including Virginia, Maryland, Kentucky, and Tennessee, as well as six states in the north. The American Colonization Society received funding from the federal government as well as from private donations.

Unlike the abolitionists, the colonizationists generally held that African Americans should be segregated socially and culturally from White Americans. Some colonizationists held that White America would never be willing to accept a racially integrated society. Others held that African Americans were naturally inferior to White people, and thus could not ever be truly equal. In arguing for an end to slavery, many colonizationists worried more about the impact on White society than on the enslaved African and African American individuals. Whatever their stance, colonizationists advocated sending emancipated slaves to Africa (from which many were removed by several generations) to colonies—such as Liberia and Sierra Leone—established by British and American missionaries. By 1843, over 4,000 African Americans, many formerly enslaved, moved to Liberia. Another 10,000 would join them in the 1840s and 1850s, and in 1847, Liberia declared its independence from the United States. Colonizationists argued for emancipation of African Americans, but not for integration: they offered an answer to the concern of many White Southerners that emancipation would create a permanently subordinate and dependent African American population that could never be integrated into the polity.

In 1834, a group of Lane students, led by radical abolitionist and 30-year-old Lane student Theodore Weld, challenged both colonization and racial segregation and formed an antislavery society at Lane. While this move was controversial enough, the "Lane rebels," as they became known, stirred up a hornet's nest when they began to mingle freely with the free Black community in Cincinnati. In a society built upon racial segregation, this action was a step too far. Lyman Beecher warned the men to be cautious of "social intercourse according to character, irrespective of color," because, while this perspective was morally fair, it was also dangerous.[16] The Lane trustees were less diplomatic. They demanded that the rebels cease their interracial activities and disband the antislavery society. Weld and his group refused and defected from Lane for the Oberlin Collegiate Institute, soon to become Oberlin College, which was one of the first racially integrated colleges in the country. By the end of the year, ninety-five of the one-hundred-and-three students at Lane had decided not to return the following year; seventy-five students specifically left the seminary in protest against the trustees' actions. While Lyman Beecher did not take a position on the controversy (in fact, he was out of town when the conflict unfolded), he—and by extension Catharine—was embroiled in the controversy, nonetheless. Branded a radical and an abolitionist—at the time a dangerous label—Lyman's local reputation in Cincinnati and national reputation as well were damaged. So too Catharine Beecher suffered by association, an irony given her refusal to take a public position on abolition or virtually any other political movement.

But Catharine Beecher was on thin ice in Cincinnati even without the Lane rebellion. Her stance on westerners, as expressed in her speeches and writings on education in the early 1830s, offended and insulted her potential donors. Westerners suffered for a lack of schools, Beecher wrote, and the entire country was subject to "deplorable ignorance."[17] Here her ego undermined her professional success. By implying that she had a "magical educational formula" that would save the people of the West Beecher alienated her friends by suggesting they were her inferiors.[18] But this was not the only issue that concerned Beecher; she worried that schools insufficiently linked Christianity and education. In the twentieth century, education became more secular when the Supreme Court banned school-sponsored prayer in public schools as a violation of the First Amendment. In Catharine Beecher's time, however, Christianity was part of the dominant American culture. Beecher believed that a proper education included ethics, which was inexorably linked to religion. To promote her educational plan, Beecher argued for a brand of eastern imperialism where the values and institutions that had been well-established in towns like Litchfield and Hartford should be transplanted to the west. Her presumption of Eastern, Protestant superiority did not only apply to Native Americans, whom many White Americans agreed needed to be "civilized"—a process that involved indigenous peoples being stripped of their heritage and re-made into a White, European model—and assimilated into American society. No, Beecher also claimed that westerners of European descent required moral and cultural refinement. Beecher's position was an extension of her father's stance that the institutions of the east—particularly Presbyterianism—should be transplanted to the west.

Lyman Beecher's entire life's work and his particular interest in revivalism reflected his desire to spread his eastern-based religion throughout the nation. Lyman was explicit about this goal, arguing that western settlers possessed "limited means of education," and advocating "the importance of introducing the social and religious principles of New England among them."[19] He disseminated these thoughts in a speech he delivered several times and published in 1835 under the title *A Plea for the West*. Like her father, Catharine too argued that the west would benefit from an eastern educational system, stating explicitly that the eastern regions of the country were intellectually and morally superior to the others.

The Beechers' tone and approach did not sit well with their Cincinnati friends and neighbors. Some of them, like James Hall, the editor of the *Western Monthly Magazine* and Dr. Daniel Drake—a prominent town father, known as "the Franklin of Cincinnati" for his varied accomplishments and philanthropic contributions—published rebuttals to the Beechers' writings on the West. Hall and Drake were offended by the suggestion that westerners were intellectually and culturally inferior to their eastern counterparts. In fact, Drake—who was born in the east but educated in Cincinnati—argued exactly the opposite. In an essay entitled *Discourse on the History, Character, and Prospects of the West*, Drake urged western communities to create their own institutions and values, unburdened by the corrupt and pretentious influences of the east.

Lines were drawn between the Beechers on the one side and Drake and Hall on the other. Not surprisingly, the Beechers—newcomers to the Queen City and proponents of arguments that were offensive to those who had lived there with pride for some time—were on the losing side. The Beechers became social pariahs and Catharine's quest to raise the $15,000 she sought for the Western Female Institute among the Cincinnati elite failed.

The lack of funding was the central problem, but other factors doomed the Western Female Institute, including Catharine Beecher's lack of attention to the school. Principal Mary Dutton reported on funding, enrollment, and staffing problems but Beecher was resistant to taking an active role in running the school and dismissed Dutton's entreaties. It did not help matters that Beecher was away from Cincinnati, traveling the Northeast seeking out "missionary teachers" to help spread her educational plans in the west. Beecher received national attention for her lectures. But she was not able to actually enroll any of the young women who were interested in a teaching career out west because her school was finally forced to close its doors in 1837.

Beecher's career as an education pioneer was hardly over. While we do not know how she felt about the Western Female Institute closing, her actions suggest that she had already placed her career priorities elsewhere. As we will see, her experiences in Cincinnati would influence her writings on slavery and womanhood. She would also experience a second—and more successful—attempt at enacting her plans for education in the west in the 1840s. But first, she made a national name for herself in a series of publications and speeches on reform and domesticity. These would afford Beecher the national platform she needed to put her education goals into action. They also would expand her repertoire and influence well beyond the schoolhouse door.

Notes

1 As quoted in Daniel Walker Howe, *What Hath God Wrought: The Transformation of America, 1815–1848* (New York: Oxford University Press, 2007), 139.
2 Kathryn Kish Sklar, *Catharine Beecher: A Study in American Domesticity* (New York: W.W. Norton & Company, 1976), 107.
3 Sklar, 107–108.
4 As quoted in John A. Jakle, "Cincinnati in the 1830s: A Cognitive Map of Traveler's Landscape Impressions," *Environmental Review* 3:2 (Spring 1979), 2.
5 Catharine Beecher, *Educational Reminiscences and Suggestions* (New York: J.B. Ford and Company, 1874), 59.
6 Catharine Beecher to Harriet Beecher (Stowe), April 17, 1832, in *Autobiography, Correspondence, Etc. of Lyman Beecher, D.D.*, vol. II, Charles Beecher, ed. (New York: Harper & Brother Publishers, 1865), Vol. II, 267, retrieved from https://www.hathitrust.org/.
7 Milton Allan Rugoff, *The Beechers: An American Family in the Nineteenth-Century* (New York: Harper & Row, 1981), 172.

8 Lyman Beecher, *A Plea for the West* (Cincinnati: Truman and Smith, 1835), 72.
9 Catharine Beecher, *An Essay on the Education of Female Teachers, for the United States* in Shirley Nelson Kersey, *Classics in the Education of Girls and Women* (Metuchen, NJ: Scarecrow Press, 1981), 292.
10 C. Beecher, *An Essay on the Education of Female Teachers*, 292.
11 Ibid.
12 Ibid.
13 C. Beecher, *An Essay on the Education of Female Teachers*, 293.
14 Charles Edward Stowe, *The Life of Harriet Beecher Stowe: Compiled from Her Letters and Journals* (Boston: Houghton, Mifflin, and Company, 1890), 84.
15 Charles Edward Stowe, *The Life of Harriet Beecher Stowe*, 86.
16 Lyman Beecher, *Autobiography, Correspondence, Etc. of Lyman Beecher, D.D.*, vol. II, ed. Charles Beecher (New York: Harper & Brother Publishers, 1865), Vol. II, 325, retrieved from https://www.hathitrust.org/.
17 C. Beecher, *An Essay on the Education of Female Teachers*, 16.
18 Ruggoff, 174.
19 Sklar, 116.

4
BEECHER'S CONSERVATISM

By the time that the Western Female Institute closed its doors in 1837 Catharine Beecher had taken a firmly conservative position on social reform, even as many of her peers were becoming more radical. The 1830s and 1840s were to the nineteenth-century what the 1960s were to the twentieth century: a period of great reform ferment. The technological advances of the Market Revolution resulted in economic booms for cities such as Cincinnati, and the Beechers' experience there served to illuminate a pivotal moment in American history—years of tremendous social and political upheaval which highlighted the Beechers' trials during this time. It was also during this era that women began to demand a more public role. Under Jacksonian Democracy suffrage was extended to most White men but excluded women and minorities. Denied a political voice through the ballot, White women exerted their political power through petitions. This strategy was particularly significant when the government attacked the rights of Native Americans. In his 1829 State of the Union address, President Andrew Jackson called for the removal of Native American tribes east of the Mississippi River to lands in the west. A group of women under the leadership of Catharine Beecher petitioned to stop Indian Removal and it was this experience that would shape Catharine Beecher's vociferous argument for women's domestic roles and her belief that moral suasion, and not political action, were the most effective ways for women to enact change.

While some white settlers started to move west even during the Revolution, their numbers were low until after the War of 1812. That conflict, between the United States and Great Britain grew out of British refusal to respect American independence in trade on the high seas. Furthermore, the United States government viewed British alliances with Native Americans in the American west as

DOI: 10.4324/b23305-5

threatening to their interests. The British would use these alliances during the war, enlisting Native Americans to fight on their side. While this strategy garnered some successes—saving Canada for the British for example—in the end, the US won the war and any protections the Native Americans enjoyed against Euro-American encroachment on their lands were now gone.

Following the war, the United States government actively encouraged westward expansion, seeing it as a boon for the strength and financial health of the federal government, who would be selling the lands to the settlers. By the 1830s, politicians, journalists, and other arbiters of American culture, such as ministers, began to develop a philosophy justifying the move westward—rooted in a current of American thought that went back to the seventeenth century and animates foreign policy still today—that the United States was formed out of a moral imperative to spread certain ideals throughout the continent and eventually the world. This "manifest destiny," as it would come to be known in the 1840s, justified westward expansion, encroachment on Native American lands, and White supremacy throughout the nineteenth-century and beyond.

As part of this imperial destiny the United States government pursued treaties with Native Americans and when that did not work, they went to war with the nations and, in some cases, forcibly removed tribes from the lands they had claimed for centuries. In other situations, tribes that had settled on new lands after being pushed out of their original lands in the East were forced to move again to satisfy the land needs of White settlers. State governments got in on the action as well, sponsoring the construction of road, canals, and eventually railroads, which would contribute to expansion westward as well.

Meanwhile, lands in the Southwestern United States—Georgia, Alabama, and Mississippi—had become newly desirable to White settlers as the cotton gin made cotton a lucrative commodity. Settlers coveted these ideal cotton-growing lands, even though large parts of these territories were claimed by five Native American nations—Cherokee, Choctaw, Cree, Chickasaw, and Seminole.

These Indigenous nations had already made accommodations to the encroachments of the United States onto their lands and into their cultures. The so-called Civilized Tribes had embraced European agricultural practices, settling and cultivating their lands. A number of Cherokees in Georgia grew cotton in their fields, and 8 percent of Cherokee landowners also owned enslaved African Americans. Many of their members spoke English, had converted to Christianity, and attended US schools run by Christian missionaries. Some intermarried with Whites, who were adopted into the Cherokee nation. The Cherokee also had a written language and a formal constitution. These assimilationist practices were an attempt by Native Americans to appease White Americans and, they hoped, ensure that the tribe could maintain their culture and lands.

But in the end, Southern Native Americans were victims of American racism and land hunger. Throughout the 1810s and 1820s, the federal government forced treaties on those groups that were willing to negotiate away their ancestral lands in exchange for land farther west. The Cherokee, Chocktaw, and Chickasaws all ceded lands in an attempt to retain some of their ancestral territory, although few people actually moved. The Creeks and Seminoles, however, were not willing to sign away their rights and waged war to protect their lands. By the mid-1820s the United States government had acquired three-fourths of Alabama and Florida, one-third in Tennessee, one-fifth of Georgia and Mississippi, and lands in Kentucky and North Carolina. It was white settler's conflicts with the Cherokee Nation in Georgia, however, that drew the greatest national attention and led to one of the most shameful episodes in American history.

Georgia settler's demand for land continued and even accelerated by the late 1820s. First, these lands became more desirable to Georgia for cotton growing and even more valuable when gold was discovered on Cherokee land in 1829. By this point, the Cherokee resisted ceding any more of their lands and Georgia insisted that the federal government make good on its compact to remove them. The administrations of James Monroe and John Quincy Adams hoped to negotiate more treaties with Native Americans but when Andrew Jackson took office, the federal drive for negotiation ended.

Negotiating with the government by no means dictated fair treatment. For example, the Cherokees agreed to cede lands in exchange for other lands and a recognition of sovereignty on the part of the Federal Government. But after gold was recognized on the Cherokees' new land, the state of Georgia reclaimed the land and refused to recognize Cherokee sovereignty. The Georgia legislature also took rights *away* from the Cherokee, including the right to testify against Whites in court. Cherokees also were forbidden by law from mining gold. The Cherokee sued the state of Georgia on the grounds that they were a sovereign nation, and not subject to the state's laws. Lawyers for the State counter argued that the Cherokee were not their own autonomous nation because they lacked a constitution and centralized government. The case went all the way up to the Supreme Court, which eventually declared that the Cherokee did have sovereign rights that the state of Georgia was bound to respect.

This victory was fleeting, though. When Andrew Jackson—who, as an Army General, was involved both in treaty- and war-making with the Native Americans—became president in 1829, the situation for Native Americans became grave. In 1830, Jackson pushed his Indian Removal Act through Congress. The Act gave Jackson the power to negotiate treaties with Native Americans who lived east of the Mississippi River to relocate them to lands to the west. At the time, few Americans foresaw that the nation would spread to these lands. Technically, the choice to relocate was voluntary, but the tribes were strongly coerced—sometimes at the end of a gun—to accept the government's offer.

Jackson's Indian Removal Act became law, with heart wrenching results for Native Americans. Jackson justified Indian Removal by claiming it would protect Native Americans who could not feasibly maintain sovereign nations within the United States' borders. He also argued that moving the Indians west would protect their lives and culture from White encroachment. But critics of Removal—and there were many—saw it as a plain and simple land grab. Indeed, even before Jackson took office, a vigorous protest movement arose in response to Indian Removal both among legislators and the general public. This opposition was especially pronounced among evangelical Christians. Their myriad periodicals such as the *Christian Advocate and Journal*, *New York Observer*, and *Boston Recorder* published editorials declaiming Indian Removal and accusing the federal government of blatantly breaking treaties and violating the laws of man and God by exploiting Christians. As they saw it, the government had made a deal with the Cherokee that if they adhered to American economic practices (such as farming) and converted to Christianity, they would be left alone.

The organized opposition to Indian Removal was the most intense protest drive in the United States to that point. As Vice President Martin Van Buren remembered twenty years later: "a more persevering opposition to a public measure had scarcely ever been made."[1] Christian missionaries were especially active in the protests and petition drives against the Removal Act. At their helm was missionary Jeremiah Evarts, an officer of the American Board of Commissioners for Foreign Missions, an organization which worked to convert Indigenous people to Protestant Christianity. Missionaries like Evarts were horrified at the government's actions against the Indigenous tribes, particularly those who had converted to Christianity. In the summer of 1829, Evarts' collection of writings against Indian Removal, entitled *The "William Penn" Essays*, was, by one estimate, read by half a million Americans. Demand for these political essays reached a pitch not seen since the American Revolution.

In addition to publishing these essays, Evarts lobbied Congress on behalf of Native Americans and sponsored protest and petition drives. Petition drives against Removal took place all around the United States, from churches to college campuses to public meetings called by town and city officials. Evarts also organized a special drive to enlist women petitioners. To head this drive he chose a well-respected, nationally known Christian woman: Catharine Beecher.

In 1828, Beecher was vacationing in Boston, when Jeremiah Evarts approached her about Indian Removal. Women, Evarts told Beecher, could protest and save the Cherokee from their fate. The two returned to Hartford and started a petition drive with the intent of inundating Congress with signatures of women opposed to Indian Removal. Beecher took the lesson she had learned in raising money in Hartford about the power of women's activism and applied it to a national cause. Her strategy was particularly female in that she called on the idea of women's moral superiority and their tradition of benevolent work to save Native Americans. In the same way that modern women's organizations such as Moms Demand Action and Mothers Against Drunk Driving emphasize the role of women in protecting children, Beecher told her readers that it was up to women to save the "helpless" Cherokee. Sympathy for these people was futile, Beecher wrote. Instead, it was up to women to sway the opinions of friends, family, and acquaintances, and effect legislation.

As Beecher had discovered in Hartford, involvement of women in politics and fundraising was hardly unprecedented. Middle-class women were very involved in Protestant revivals and the attendant fundraising and political work that went along with evangelical Protestantism in the antebellum period. Women often brought their male family members into the church and participated in raising money for the charitable works that came out of the religious institutions. Women also organized and held bazaars, charitable drives, and other fundraisers. Christian women had been working in charitable organizations, including those that ministered to Native Americans, and Beecher called on these women to join the petition drive in a mass mailing of a "Circular Addressed to the Benevolent Ladies of the United States," which she also published on Christmas Day 1829 in the magazine *Christian Advocate and Journal*. The Circular asked for recipients to forward it along, to sponsor petitions, and to hold meetings raising awareness of the campaign against removal. The Ladies' Circular was extremely effective. Over 1,400 women from all over the United States signed petitions to Congress opposing Cherokee removal.

But the escalation of women's petitioning in response to the Indian Removal Act represented a new and audacious move on the part of women's political involvement in the United States. Prior to this point, women had engaged in petition drives but generally to local governments, not to the United States Congress, and in some cases, under the rubric of a male representative. Indeed, an organized protest by women was so novel and radical that Beecher and her Hartford friends decided the best course was to remain anonymous. They signed the petition anonymously and mailed it from four different cities, so it would not be associated directly with the women of Hartford. Beecher even swore the printer to secrecy. While Beecher would later claim authorship of the petition, at the time she struggled to keep her involvement a secret. As with other stressful situations, the strain overtook Beecher. She was overcome with physical pain and confusion. Her departure for Boston in the winter of 1829–1830—following Zilpah Grant's humiliating rebuff of Hartford Seminary—stemmed in part from the stress she felt over keeping secret her authorship of the Ladies' Circular.

In the end, the campaign against removal was unsuccessful. Despite the unprecedented outcry—hundreds of petitions filed and countless sermons, pamphlets, and essays against Jackson's Indian policy—the southeastern tribes were removed by force to lands beyond the Mississippi River. The outcry did have an impact on Congress—the bill passed the house by only five votes, and the Senate by nine and congressional support for the bill was limited to the South. The Cherokee, with the backing and outcry of their supporters, took their case to the Supreme Court, and the Court found in their favor, ruling that the state of

Georgia had no jurisdiction over Native American lands. But the Court's decision notwithstanding, Native Americans were removed anyway. Their forced relocation to Indian Territory in 1838 is popularly known as the Trail of Tears, because it resulted in thousands of Native deaths from exposure, starvation, and disease.

Despite the terrible outcome, the case against removal was not for naught. In some ways, the protests and petition informed the abolition movement which took steam in the 1830s and had many of the same members. For women in particular, involvement in the petition drive whet their appetites for and gave credence to their participation in matters political. It also gave them skills and networks to pursue their political battles, particularly in the abolition movement. But the leader of the women's petition drive, Catharine Beecher did not join her friends and sisters in the movement against slavery. Ironically, the same woman who wrote the Ladies' Circular and urged her fellow female Americans to take a public role and voice against removal urged the opposite when it came to the movement against slavery.

For many reform women the success of the Ladies' Circular in mobilizing women established political skills that would later be utilized by women in the antislavery and woman's rights movements. For Beecher, however, the public criticisms directed at anti-removalists was devastating. She reversed her views on women's political engagement, arguing instead that women should influence men to petition but refrain from political activity, themselves. This rhetorical recoil also influenced Beecher's views on antislavery. She became a critic of immediate emancipation. Instead—like her father—Beecher endorsed the American Colonization Society, which encouraged African Americans to migrate to Africa rather than integrate into White society.

While technically part of the antislavery movement, colonization was controversial from the start. Many Blacks argued that culturally they were American and should be allowed to remain in the United States to fight for equality. White reformers also debated the merit of colonization, contending that only immediate emancipation would rid the country of slavery. These arguments would lay the groundwork for the abolition movement.

By the 1830s, the movement for abolition was gaining steam among American Christian reformers. Abolitionists such as Arthur and Lewis Tappan, Theodore Dwight Weld, William Lloyd Garrison, Angelina and Sarah Grimke, Lucretia Mott, and Frederick Douglass published editorials and spoke publicly against slavery. The main strategy employed by these reformers was moral suasion, which used arguments reflecting Christian morality to reason that slaveholders should willingly change their ways. While moral suasion rarely worked, the growing presence of abolition in both print and the public forum signaled a change in American politics.

Catharine Beecher's adopted home state of Ohio was not impervious to the impact of the abolition movement, as the 1836 race riots demonstrated.

Cincinnati was emblematic both of the growing movement for abolition and the opposition to it among mainstream Americans. In 1837, Catharine Beecher also took a stand. Perhaps surprisingly to a modern reader, the stand she took was in opposition to the gathering abolitionist moment. Beecher published an essay in which she forcefully argued against a role for women in the abolitionist movement. While other members of Beecher's family—most notably her sister Harriet Beecher Stowe, author or *Uncle Tom's Cabin*, and her brother Henry Ward Beecher, a congregationalist minister—would eventually choose to take a more radical stance toward ending slavery, she remained steadfast in her belief that women should not be involved in this movement. The catalyst for Beecher's Essay was the public abolitionist activities of two White, Southern sisters Angelina and Sarah Grimke.

The Grimke sisters were particularly powerful advocates for abolition. They grew up in the South, part of a wealthy, South Carolina slaveholding family, and were the only White, Southern women to represent the abolitionist movement. The Grimke family was Southern aristocracy. Their family owned two plantations and a townhouse in Charleston. They also owned numerous slaves, putting them in the small percentage of white southerners who owned twenty slaves or more. So, when they characterized slavery as brutal, exploitative not only of the labor, bodies, and fortunes of slaves but also damaging to the White slaveholders by compromising their morality, they were especially convincing because they had come up in the system that they grew to reject.

The Grimkes came to abolition through religion. The sisters were twelve years apart and, in some senses, Sarah acted more as a mother or aunt to Angelina and influenced her younger sister's religious and social views considerably. Sarah, and not long after Angelina, came to believe that owning slaves was sinful. Growing up in a slaveholding family, Angelina grew disturbed at the daily evidence before her of slavery's brutality. The sounds of overseers whipping slaves, the sight of scars and wounds incurred by enslaved people as a result of these whippings, and the general injustice of holding people in bondage, had a devastating impact on the young Angelina.

Grimke sought answers and explanations in the Church. As a teenager, Angelina had turned away from the apologist Episcopalian faith of her family and converted to the Presbyterian Church, of which she became a dedicated and devout member. Before long, however, Angelina found that the Church's stance on slavery was far more conservative than her own emerging views. While Angelina was coming to think slavery was an evil that needed to be eradicated, the Presbyterian Church was finding ways to accommodate the peculiar institution, asking slaveholders to treat their slaves well, but not demanding outright abolition. In 1829, Angelina broke with the Presbyterian Church (or rather, the Church, fed up with Angelina's outspoken opposition to slavery, broke with Angelina). Angelina had also worn out her welcome with her family, weary of Angelina's criticism of their extravagant lifestyle and particularly of their attachment to slavery. At this point, Sarah Grimke had moved to Philadelphia and was attending Orthodox Quaker meetings in that city. Angelina joined Sarah both in the city of Brotherly Love and in the Quaker Meeting. But the Grimke sisters found the Quaker community in Philadelphia confining and Angelina continued to search for some purpose to guide her life and actions. She came to find it in abolition.

Abolition was still very much a fringe movement in the early 1830s. Most antislavery agitation was directed toward colonization, a movement which claimed the Beechers as adherents. Colonizationists argued for emancipation but with the expectation that newly freed slaves would emigrate to colonies in Africa. But the movement for abolition was gaining steam, given a boost by the full abolition of slavery in the British colonies in 1833. Philadelphia had a small but active abolitionist community, and Angelina made tentative steps to join them in 1834, attending meetings of the Female Anti-Slavery Society, reading abolitionist tracts, and going to abolitionist lectures. In 1835, Angelina flung herself full into the movement. This leap was precipitated by a private letter that Angelina wrote to abolitionist William Lloyd Garrison in 1835 in support of his immediatist stance toward ending slavery.

Garrison, the editor of the abolitionist newspaper *The Liberator*, and founder of the American Anti-Slavery Society, had been stirring controversy for over four years demanding an immediate end to slavery and the emancipation of all American slaves. This outspoken stance, along with Garrison's unwavering political radicalism—he eschewed both political parties, refused to vote, critiqued the Constitution as a proslavery document, eventually brining a copy of it in public, calling it "an Agreement with Hell," and demanded full equality for African Americans—garnered derision from most Americans, even those who were inclined to oppose slavery.

And for those who were not so inclined, Garrison and others who demanded immediate abolition were viewed as a dangerous threat to the racial and economic status quo. In the 1830s, anti-abolition mobs attacked abolitionist and African American targets, including homes, churches, businesses, and newspaper offices as well as abolitionist meetings and lectures in northern and northeastern cities. Prominent abolitionists were directly targeted—including the Quaker poet John Greenleaf Whitter who was stoned by a Massachusetts mob in retribution for his abolitionist writings, and Garrison himself, who was physically attacked at a meeting of the Boston Female Anti-Slavery Society in October of 1835.

Angelina Grimke was simultaneously alarmed by these violent acts and spurred to action as a result of them. In August of 1835, she wrote a private letter to William Lloyd Garrison in response to Garrison's call for Bostonians to repudiate mob violence, especially in preparation for a visit of the famed British abolitionist—George Thompson—to the city. In the letter, Grimke expressed support for Garrison's position and for abolitionism in general, exclaiming it "a cause worth dying for."² Angelina did not intend her letter to be published—she was embracing the abolitionist cause, but was not yet quite ready to be its spokesperson. But the canny Garrison saw an opportunity in making the daughter of a wealthy slaveholding family a spokesperson for the cause In September, Garrison published Grimke's letter in *The Liberator*. Other abolitionist publications further circulated Angelina's words, catapulting her onto the stage as an ardent and yet reluctant spokesperson for the abolitionist cause.

Angelina's unintended affiliation with Garrison brought her the opprobrium of the Quaker community of Philadelphia and of course her family in South Carolina. Even her bosom sister Sarah was horrified at Angelina's alignment with the radical editor (though Sarah came around, eventually taking an important and active role herself in the abolitionist movement as an agent for the American Anti-Slavery Society). But rather than silencing her, the criticism—along with the vociferous support of the abolitionist movement—steeled her to further action. In September of 1836, Grimke published her *Appeal to the Christian Women of the South*, inviting other Southern White women to join her in the fight to abolish slavery.

Grimke's *Appeal*, like Beecher's anonymous appeal against Indian Removal, was aimed at women like herself. But unlike the reform-minded women that Beecher had hoped to reach, Grimke's focus was a group not inclined to politics or to reform—the daughters, wives, and sisters of the slaveholding South. Grimke recognized this point and tried to relate to them as a friend and neighbor, which she could do effectively since she had been raised in this society. Grimke argued that women—whom she believed were the moral leaders of their families and society—had a particular role to play in the movement against the immoral system of slavery. Indeed, Grimke appealed to her readers as both moral beings and mothers when she asked if slave traders were excluded from polite society because

> even you shrink back from the idea of associating with those who make their fortunes by trading in the bodies and souls of men, women, and children? whose daily work is to break human hearts, by tearing wives from their husbands, and children from their parents?³

Why, Grimke continued, should these men be rejected when those that hire them, in many cases the women's husband's, were respected? This tactic—known as moral suasion—was frequently used in antislavery writings of the era and Grimke masterfully argued that women's natural virtue placed the responsibility of highlighting the sin of slavery with them.

Given the parallels between Grimke's arguments against slavery and those that Beecher made against Indian Removal, one might expect that Catharine Beecher would have been very sympathetic to the abolitionist's arguments about women's role in ending slavery. But scarred by the earlier battle, Beecher had little interest in entering another effort to advocate a public, political role for women. Instead, Beecher published an argument against Angelina Grimke in her 1837 *Essay on Slavery and Abolitionism, with Reference to the Duty of American Females*. In the essay, Beecher laid out her arguments against the abolitionist movement in general as well as the proper role of American women in political discourse and activity. She took offense at Grimke's assumption that northern women were unfamiliar with the abolition movement. Christian women universally agreed slavery was wrong, she insisted, but most of these women would support gradual abolition, not the radical politics of the Grimkes. Beecher scolded Grime,

> ...there is no necessity for using any influence with northern ladies, in order that they may adopt your *principles* on the subject of slavery; for they hold them in common with yourself, and it would seem unwise, and might prove irritating, to approach them as if they hold opposite sentiments.[4]

Beecher's issues with Grimke's essay, however, only began with her attempt to educate northern women. Beecher opposed the politicization of the abolition movement in general and women's involvement specifically.

The *Essay* illustrates the complexity of Catharine Beecher's position on women in public. Beecher was burned by the criticism from the advocates of Indian Removal for her anonymous petition drive against their cause and it shaped her position about women's role in politics. But at the same time, by publishing a 152-page essay arguing against abolitionism, Beecher was indeed taking a political stance and engaging actively in political culture.

The major difference between Beecher's stance and Grimke's was that Grimke's position was radical and Beecher's was conservative. Indeed, Beecher's main stated reason for publishing her essay was to show a male friend why he should not join the abolitionist movement. Here, Beecher was taking the position that her moral stance as a woman permitted her to advise male acquaintances on their political activities. But toward the end of the essay Beecher also focused on upbraiding women like the Grimke sisters for taking a public role in their advocacy for abolition. Angelina Grimke, who had once admired Catharine Beecher, was angered by Beecher's rebuke. Grimke confided to a friend, "I do not know how I shall find language strong enough to express my indignation at the view she takes of woman's character and duty."[5] For Angelina Grimke abolition was not only a moral right, but also her career. And under her influence the movement was growing.

Catharine Beecher published her *Essay on Slavery and Abolitionism* amid a year of significant progress for the abolitionist movement. While still a radical movement, abolition was gaining more adherents and more of an institutional framework. The number of antislavery societies tripled from 1835 to 1836, growing from around 300 groups to almost 1000. These included all-male societies and several female societies after the model of the Boston Female Anti-Slavery Society, founded in 1832. The movement had an active speakers' circuit, which the Grimke sisters joined, serving as important first-hand opponents of the peculiar institution. And in 1836, abolitionists embarked on an effective petition campaign against the "gag rule" imposed by the Senate (under pressure from Southern members), wherein they refused to entertain any petitions pertaining to abolition.

And in early 1837, New York hosted the first American female antislavery convention. Among the delegates to the convention were some of the most well-known American female reformers of the time: Philadelphia Quaker Lucretia Mott, abolitionist Maria Weston Chapman from Massachusetts along with Beecher's friend Lydia Maria Child and the Grimke sisters, "representing" South Carolina, the only slaveholding state with delegates at the convention.

In June, following the convention, Angelina and Sarah Grimke embarked on a grueling lecture tour of New England, speaking in front of audiences of hundreds of people about the horrors of slavery and their first-hand experience with it. The Grimkes' activities placed them at the intersection of two very radical stances—the proposal that slavery was evil and must be abolished; and the suggestion that women should have an active role in public life. Indeed, the second was possibly the more radical since even many of those who agreed with abolition disagreed that women should be its messengers. Even many audiences friendly to abolition responded negatively to the Grimke's lectures, particularly those in front of mixed audiences of men and women. While there was a role for women lecturing exclusively to other women in the 1830s, the idea of women speaking in public in front of a "promiscuous" audience, one that included gentlemen as well as ladies, flew in the face of the strict gender mores of the antebellum middle-class. In some New England towns, ministers refused to publicize the Grimke's talks to their parishioners or to allow them to speak from their pulpits.

Beecher registered her own disapproval of the Grimkes' activities in her *Essay on Slavery and Abolitionism*. Beecher was clear about her influence. Her essay was subtitled "Addressed to A.M. Grimke." Beecher explained, "Miss Grimke's Address was presented, and the information communicated of her intention to visit the North, for the purpose of using her influence among northern ladies to induce them to unite with Abolition Societies."[6] What began as a personal letter to Grimke developed into the published essay.

A good portion of Beecher's *Essay on Slavery and Abolition* was a critique of abolition in general. Beecher took a centrist stance on the matter that was in line with the stance of a much larger proportion of Americans than the abolitionist movement was. Beecher's stance shows the spectrum of the antislavery approach in the 1830s. Like the radical abolitionists who demanded an immediate end to slavery for African Americans, Beecher argued that slavery was evil and had to be ended, but as a Colonizationist she claimed that this should be instigated by Southern slaveholders coming around to the antislavery position as opposed to abolitionist agitation. Colonizationists like Beecher did not see a place for African Americans in the United States and argued for forced emigration of newly freed slaves to colonies in Africa such as Liberia and Sierra Leone.

Like other mainstream reformers, Beecher also took issue with the tactics of the abolitionist movement, arguing that the cause was just but the measures to achieve it were so shrill and provocative as to turn people away from the movement. Indeed, Beecher argued that the response to abolitionists—the gag rule, the mob violence, the anti-abolitionist attacks on the press—were in fact sought after by abolitionists in order to publicize their cause. But, she claimed, these attempts backfired, turning moderate Americans off to abolitionism rather than encouraging them to join the movement. Beecher had a personal stake in her argument against abolition. Her defensive stance was surely rooted in part in the anti-abolitionist riots that wrought Cincinnati in 1836.

In her *Essay on Slavery and Abolition*, Beecher made clear and direct reference to the events around the Cincinnati riots. For example, she took issue with the decision to establish *The Philanthropist* in Cincinnati, rather than "in a small place, where the people were of similar views, or were not exposed to dangerous popular excitements."[7] When Cincinnati leaders expressed concern about a violent reaction to the paper's presence in the city, Beecher claimed, the publisher refused to back down, insisting that "The paper must not only be printed and circulated, but it must be stationed where were the greatest probabilities that measures of illegal violence would ensue."[8] And, she concluded:

> when the evil was perpetrated, and a mob destroyed the press, then those who had urged on these measures of temptation, turned upon those who had advised and remonstrated, as the guilty authors of the violence, because, in a season of excitement, the measures adopted to restrain and control the mob, were not such as were deemed suitable and right.[9]

But if her alarm at abolitionist tactics and action spurred Beecher to write the essay, it was Angelina Grimke's arguments about women's role in the political cause that led Beecher to address it directly to her friend. In answering Grimke's claim that

> [t]he *women of the South can overthrow* this horrible system of oppression and cruelty, licentiousness, and wrong. Such appeals to your legislatures would be irresistible, for there is something in the heart of man which *will bend under moral suasion*.[10]

Beecher spelled out further her own position about women's role in the polity, one which informed her arguments about the importance of women's education as well as her crusade for domesticity upon which she would embark in subsequent decades.

In taking such a public role in the abolitionist movement, the Grimke sisters were articulating a new position for women in American society. They knew that if women were to have a significant role in politics, they must first challenge the social restrictions placed upon their gender. Sarah Grimke noted that "There are few things which present greater obstacles to the improvement and elevation of women to her appropriate sphere of usefulness and duty, than the laws which have been enacted to destroy her independence and crush her individuality." Women had had no influence in writing these laws which now limited their rights, Sarah continued. "Woman," she wrote, "has no political existence."[11] But the sisters were not content to simply write about women's inequality, they wanted action. After attending the 1837 meeting of the American Anti-Slavery Society Angelina discussed the issue with other female abolitionists, who agreed "it was time our fetters were broken." Angelina was invigorated. She wrote to her friend Jane Smith, "What an untrodden path we have entered upon!"[12] The Grimke sisters were pushing the boundaries of women's roles.

Unlike the position that both Grimke sisters were developing vis-à-vis women's role in society, Beecher took a much more conservative view. Women, she claimed, were not equal to men, but rather subordinate to them like children were subordinate to parents or students to teachers. Women should accept this subordinate role and allow their fathers and husbands to represent them in economic and political matters, Beecher argued. But they should not assume that they were either inferior to men or powerless. Rather, they should seek power through different means, to offer influence through the moral suasion of their male relations. "Woman is to win everything by peace and love," Beecher explained:

> by making herself so much respected, esteemed, and loved, that to yield to her opinions and to gratify her wishes, will be the free-will offering of the heart. But this is to be all accomplished in the domestic and social circle.[13]

To Beecher, women had no need for political influence.

Thus, unlike the Grimkes, who argued that women were entitled to gender equality, Beecher argued that women's power lay in their ability to love and be loved by men, and to exert influence through that love. Beecher based her stance on an assumption that women possessed a purity of thought and intent than men did not. In other words, women, though dependent, had a measure of independence since they were less corruptible than men. They were motivated from a position of morality and love, not from a position of venality or ambition. If they strayed in that direction, however, Beecher argued, women lose their influence: "The moment woman begins to feel the promptings of ambition, or the thirst for power" Beecher claimed, "her aegis of defense is gone."[14]

Beecher also argued that involvement in abolition would further degrade this "aegis of defense" since "it leads them into the arena of political collision, not as peaceful mediators to hush the opposing elements, but as combatants to cheer up and carry forward the measures of strife."[15] She insisted that women should not sign petitions as that removed them from their proper sphere as influencers. If they could not influence their own male relatives to sign the petitions, "then they surely are out of their place, in attempting to do it themselves."[16] A peculiar stance from the anonymous leader of the women's petition drive against Cherokee removal, but a sign of Beecher's stance on politics henceforth.

If Beecher hoped her essay would sway Grimke to her position, she was mistaken. Grimke responded with a series of letters addressed to Beecher in which she defended the abolitionist movement and spelled out her position on women's equality. Indeed, the Grimke-Beecher exchange—which included both Angelina's letters, published in *The Liberator* and *The Emancipator* in the summer of 1837 and her sister Sarah's *Letters on the Equality of the Sexes, and the Condition of Women*, published in book form in 1837—set the parameters for a central debate among American feminists that, in some cases, still has resonance today: whether to emphasize women's essential equality with men or whether to highlight the differences between the sexes as a means of achieving equal rights. Beecher clearly stood on the "difference" side—arguing that women's inherent qualities of morality, pacifism, and virtue set them apart from their husbands, fathers, and sons, and should be cultivated as a way for them to achieve status in American society. While Beecher saw their domestic role as most valuable, she also imagined a professional niche for women as teachers of young children.

The Grimkes, on the other hand, argued both that women were equal to men and that they should take a role in public in general and in the abolitionist movement specifically. The Grimkes took issue with Beecher's claim that God had created women as subordinate to men. Rather, they argued, that women were due equal rights because God had ordained that they were equal to men. "I know nothing of men's rights and women's rights; for in Christ Jesus, there is neither male nor female," Angelina chided.[17] As Angelina explained, "Human beings have *rights*, because they are *moral* beings: the rights of *all* men grow out of their moral nature; and as all men have the same moral nature, they have essentially the same rights."[18] Beecher's emphasis on difference, Grimke argued, had an adverse impact not only on women but on men as well, indeed on all of society, citing "that multifarious train of evils flowing out of the anti-Christian doctrine of masculine and feminine virtues." While men were naturalized as non-sentimental "warriors," women were relegated to ornaments and "drudges" and stripped of their essential rights, including the right to speak out against injustices such as slavery.[19] They pointed to biblical examples—Miriam, Deborah, Huldah, Anna, and the female followers of Jesus—to challenge Beecher's claim that women's influence should be confined to the domestic sphere. And to Beecher's argument that women should not engage in political debates, petitions, or other actions, but rather consent to being represented by their male relations, Grimke raised the image of the American Revolutionaries. American women, she pointed out, were in the same position as the eighteenth-century Patriots, taxed without representation, and "governed by laws which *they* had no voice in making."[20] The Grimke sisters' gender arguments would later shape the foundation of the Woman's Rights Movement.

Catharine Beecher, however, would not be persuaded. Although she must have felt vulnerable after the closure of the Western Female Institute and was depressed by the confrontation with Angelina Grimke, she was not about to modify her viewpoints. She saw no benefit in women's political action. Instead, Beecher argued that a woman's greatest influence was through domesticity. This belief reflected the values of most free people at the time. In arguing that the home—and women within it—should be revered, she linked the future of the nation with domestic virtue. Her most famous publication—*Treatise on Domestic Economy*—would reiterate these points and in doing so create a female identity that placed women at the center of American culture but on the periphery of its politics.

Notes

1 Martin Van Buren, *The Autobiography of Martin Van Buren*, ed. John C Fitzpatrick (Washington: Government Printing Officer, 1920), 288.
2 Angelina Grimke, "Slavery and the Boston riot. The following letter was written, shortly after the pro-slavery riot in Boston by Angeline E. Grimke to William Lloyd Garrison... 1835" (Boston: 1835), Library of Congress, Rare Book and Special Collections Division, Printed Ephemera Collection.
3 Angelina Grimke, *Appeal to the Christian Women of the South* (New York: American Anti-Slavery Society, 1836), 15.
4 Catharine Beecher, *An Essay on Slavery and Abolitionism* (Philadelphia: Henry Perkins, 1837), 7–8.
5 Angelina Grimke to Jane Smith, June 1837 in *Women's Rights Emerges within the Anti-Slavery Movement, 1830-1870: A Brief History with Documents*, ed. Kathryn Kish Sklar (New York: Palgrave MacMillan, 2000), 116.
6 C. Beecher, *An Essay on Slavery and Abolitionism*, 7.
7 C. Beecher, *An Essay on Slavery and Abolitionism*, 32.
8 C. Beecher, *An Essay on Slavery and Abolitionism*, 33–34.
9 C. Beecher, *An Essay on Slavery and Abolitionism*, 34.
10 A. Grimke, *Appeal to the Christian Women of the South*, 26.
11 Sarah Grimke, *Letters on the Equality of the Sexes* (Boston: Isaac Knapp, 1838), 74.
12 Angelina Grimke to Jane Smith, May 29, 1837 in *Women's Rights Emerges within the Antislavery Movement*, 111.
13 C. Beecher, *An Essay on Slavery and Abolitionism*, 101.
14 Ibid.
15 C.Beecher, *An Essay on Slavery and Abolitionism*, 103.
16 C. Beecher, *An Essay on Slavery and Abolitionism*, 105.

17 Angelina Grimke, *Letters to Catharine Beecher, In Reply to an Essay on Slavery and Abolitionism, Addressed to A.E. Grimke Revised by Author, Letter XII Human Rights Not Founded on Sex* (Boston: Isaac Knapp, 1838), 118.
18 A. Grimke, *Letters to Catharine Beecher*, 114.
19 A. Grimke, *Letters to Catharine Beecher*, 115–116.
20 A. Grimke, *Letters to Catharine Beecher*, 112.

5
DOMESTICITY

Catharine Beecher's printed debate with Angelina Grimke lasted two years and established her as an expert on the moral superiority of women. Her teaching career, however, had halted. Following the closure of the Western Female Institute in 1837, she was without a job. Few work prospects for women meant that she was once again a dependent in her father's household. At almost forty years old, Beecher's career had thus been conducted in a series of fits and starts rather than consistent accomplishments. It was also becoming clear that she preferred the excitement of opening schools to the monotony of running them. And so, as she moved away from teaching, Beecher compiled her ideas about domesticity into a series of publications, the most famous of which was an instructional book for running a home entitled *Treatise on Domestic Economy, For the Use of Young Ladies at Home and at School*. Yet, while her published works encouraged her counterparts to embrace their responsibilities as wives and mothers, Beecher possessed neither title. As a single, career woman, her place in society was ambiguous, and thus she used her writings to justify the paradoxes in her own life; she emphasized a domestic role for women that she did not personally embrace.

When Catharine Beecher first began developing her theories on domestic economy the United States was fully emersed in an industrial revolution, which would forever change technology and manufacturing and expand the economy. For example, in the West, transportation innovations such as the steamboat and the railroad made commercial farming a possibility. Americans looking for land relocated to western frontiers, embracing the ideology of manifest destiny. In 1800, the year that Beecher was born, a little more than 300,000 people lived west of the Appalachian Mountains. By 1820, that number had swelled to 2 million, and the Southern United States surpassed India as the leading cotton producer in the world. In 1836, overseas cotton sales reached $71 million. This

DOI: 10.4324/b23305-6

demand for cotton created an increased market for slaves, making the interstate slave trade a profitable business. With the 1808 ban on the international slave trade, Slave owners relied on natural reproduction—or childbearing—to increase slave populations; a situation that often led to forced copulation between slaves or rape.

Simultaneously in the North, cities grew rapidly as an explosion of factories, many of which produced southern cotton into cloth, enticed rural youth to pursue urban wage labor. Between 1820 and 1850, urban populations multiplied five times over. Goods and information also began to circulate differently. Canals, turnpikes, and railroads made it easier to move people and goods in and out of cities and innovations in the printing press meant that millions of newspapers could be printed per day and sold to the public for as little as a penny. The opportunities that these changes made available for some contributed to the development of an ideology of individualism, or the social belief that personal desires superseded—but still advanced—the needs of the many. For a white man who purchased land or took a well-paying job in an urban shop, individualism was an exercise in independence. For Catharine Beecher herein was a problem. She worried that the focus on individualism—under the guise of democracy—was corrupting society.

Beecher's fears were reiterated by ministers. As the chief critics of individualism, these men argued that by encouraging people to excel for their own good, service to the community was lost. The proposed solution was to find a model—preferably young businessmen who best exemplified the democratic values of the nation and could therefore justify capitalism—to lead the nation by exhibiting strong moral values. It was assumed that the rest of society would follow their example because these young men personified the accomplishments and social hierarchy of the newly formed middle-class.

The antebellum American middle-class was defined by income, occupation, and culture. To be middle-class meant being neither wealthy nor poor. Previous generations had referred to this economic status as "middling," but the nature of work had also changed with northern industrialization. Families no longer worked side by side at home as men left farms and independent workshops to take wage paying positions as tradesmen, merchants, and clerks in urban centers. Men working these jobs used their intellect rather than their hands, unlike their counterparts on the docks and in factories. They, along with the doctors and lawyers who also made up the middle-class, were typically able to financially support their families without the monetary contribution of their wives. This was a distinct change from Catharine Beecher's childhood, when her mother, Roxana, supplemented the family's income by boarding students and running a school out of the home. By the 1830s, society would have frowned upon the wife of a minister taking odd jobs for money. While Lyman Beecher had earned around $400 a year during Catharine's early childhood, by midcentury a typical middle-class household earned approximately $1,000 annually. This income level was unattainable for the families of manual laborers. However, unlike the modern middle-class, which is defined primarily by income level, the middle-class in the nineteenth-century was also defined by behaviors that were romanticized in popular writings such as prescriptive literature, essays, sermons, novels, and poems.

According to these authors, an integral part of middle-class ethos was the division of labor into separate spheres; men worked in public while women remained in the privacy of the home. Some modern gender philosophers emphasize the role of culture in constructing gender identity; for example, during the 1940s the colors blue and pink were assigned to boys and girls. Other theorists argue that gender identity is innate. During the nineteenth-century, however, it was believed that gender and biological sex were the same, and denoted specific characteristics. Tasks such as cleaning the home, cooking meals, and washing and mending clothing were supposed to come naturally to women, while men were more suited for business. In outlining the differences between male and female work, however, prescriptive literature sentimentalized domesticity with images of immaculate homes and smiling children. This effectively made women's labor invisible. Femininity for middle-class women and girls was defined by the embrace of certain behaviors, specifically piety, purity, domesticity, and submissiveness—referred to by historians as the culture (cult) of domesticity. The cult of domesticity linked women's roles exclusively to motherhood and nurturing the family and was reinforced by the legal doctrine of coverture, which subsumed a married woman's legal identity to her husband's. Therefore, a married woman could not manage property in her name, sue or be sued, or execute a will without her husband's permission. The cult of domesticity was also treated as a marker of respectability. A woman who personified this culture was considered a "true woman."

Critical differences in race and social class and even geographic location made true womanhood impossible for many if not most American women, however. Rural and urban White women could not be reasonably expected to fulfill the domestic demands the proponents of the cult espoused, for they also had to work a multitude of jobs to help financially support their families. In rural areas, poor women sold butter, eggs, and chickens while in cities like New York many participated in the manufacturing industry. Some worked in the factories while others took in sewing in their small, badly lit, and poorly ventilated tenement housing. With no minimum wage, no job security, and no benefits, they were often overworked and too frequently unemployed.

Most working women in the cities found themselves employed as domestic servants in the homes of the middle and upper classes. Domestic positions, which included room and board, paid better than jobs in manufacturing, but they required long days and heavy workloads. By 1850, most domestic servants were immigrant Irish women and girls who fled the Irish Potato Famine. The relationship between these Irish servants and their employers laid bare the class discrepancies of the cult of domesticity. Middle-class women who saw it as their duty to transform their servants into "ladies," often found these Irish women resistant.

Despite an Irish servant's rejection of the demands of the cult, her Whiteness made the path to "true womanhood" theoretically possible. For the enslaved African American women, no avenue to true womanhood existed. Treated as property rather than persons, they could be subjected to intense labor, beatings, rape, and separation from their children. Free African American women lived under discriminatory laws. Some eked out a living as seamstresses and laundresses, although a few did become shopkeepers, bakers, teachers, or boardinghouse owners. Perhaps most commonly, however, free Black women became domestic servants, working as cooks, laundresses, or housekeepers in the homes of white families. Unlike Irish servants, these Black women were not seen as projects to be reformed; their skin color denied them even the possibility of admittance into the cult of domesticity.

Gender was also not as fixed as proponents of the cult might lead their readers to believe. On the western frontier, the shortage of labor meant that settlers completed any task at hand. Men often did housework and women often cleared land and constructed buildings. With fewer women than men among the settlers, social events often meant men taking turns at the woman's part in dancing. Sometimes men even wore women's clothing to these dances. These reversals of gender roles were typically temporary. Yet there were people who permanently identified as members of the opposite sex. A person assigned female at birth might embrace roles typically associated with men, becoming a "female husband" and assuming legal and economic responsivities for a family. Some even married women. There were several reasons for such a choice to live as a man, including better pay in the workplace or Queer identity. Proponents of the cult of domesticity ignored outliers like these.

Catharine Beecher had been developing her own theories on women's social role since she founded the Hartford Female Seminary in 1823. In 1831 she published these ideas as *The Elements of Mental and Moral Philosophy, Founded Upon Experience, Reason and the Bible*. Based on Beecher's lectures from the Hartford Female Seminary, this volume established women as the moral guardians of the United States. She argued that salvation was social, rather than theological, and defined a moral code intended to regulate personal behavior. It was important, she contended, that people learn to recognize true virtue rather than hypocrisy. "All will agree that virtue consists of acting in the general good of society, though there may be much difference of opinion, as to the best mode to be pursued," she wrote. The danger was not in people who tried to be good and sometimes failed, but in

> [...] persons who claim to be consulting the best interests of society [but] are making strenuous efforts to prevent the operation of this fear. They deliberately aim to convince their fellow men that there is not so much danger in indulging selfishness, and the practice of evil, as they are taught to believe, by those who interpret the Bible like other books, and maintain that it teaches nothing but truth.[1]

Beecher was concerned that society's leaders were held to standards far different than the rest of Americans. In this assertion, her bitterness toward religion was evident.

Beecher's experience with Christian ministers had shown her that the very men instructing others on how to live often violated the standards they preached. Her proposed solution was that everyone should embrace one quality, self-sacrifice, for it was through self-sacrifice that moral superiority could best be demonstrated. Her argument was clearly influenced by the ideas of the Second Great Awakening, which challenged the notion of predestination—a doctrine that some people were fated to reach Heaven while others were not. The proponents of the Second Great Awakening argued that salvation was not fated; it was up to the individual. They insisted a sinner could always be reformed. Beecher built on this theology, arguing that salvation was also based on influencing the greater societal good. "Again," she wrote, "it is the universal experience of mankind, that benevolent self-sacrifice for the good of others, is one of the most interesting of all traits of character, and best calculated to promote grateful obedience, and admiring imitation."² In building this case, she claimed that morality superseded piety. The difference may seem subtle, but in making this transition Beecher challenged the absolute power of ministers to regulate right and wrong by placing the responsibility on ordinary people. But if not ministers, who would supervise the morality of the American people? Beecher had an answer for this too: women. She claimed that, as the more virtuous of the sexes, it was up to women to serve as examples of benevolence while men combated the sins of capitalism. In building the argument of her book around this theory, she used the cult of domesticity to empower women, arguing womanhood was synonymous with integrity.

The Elements of Mental and Moral Philosophy did not make Catharine Beecher rich or famous. She published it anonymously at her own expense and the public reception was varied. Nonetheless, this work was an important turning point for her and boosted her confidence as a writer. When she moved to Cincinnati the following year, Beecher began promoting her cultural theories through articles published in the regional literary journal *Western Monthly Magazine*.

Beecher had two literary objectives in 1832: first, she wanted to create a textbook on domestic economy that could be adopted in girls' schools, and second, she hoped to create a steady income for herself through her writing. As a single woman, Beecher's earning potential was limited. There was little money in teaching, and she knew from her experiences at both the Hartford Female Seminary and the Western Female Institute that a school without an endowment had little chance of sustaining itself. Writing was one of the few socially acceptable options available to her to supplement her income. In this, Beecher was not alone. During this era, many women turned to writing to support themselves and their families At midcentury, most White women were literate, and this made them writers as well as consumers of literature. Some literary women wrote novels, but others made a living by writing advice manuals directed at other women. These manuals—including Lydia Maria Child's 1829 *The American Frugal Housewife*—described a new domestic role for middle-class women without challenging other, more traditional gender roles. Catharine Beecher was working on a different theory, one that elevated women as the moral educators of the nation.

In Beecher's view, women's differences from men needed to be emphasized in order to stress their unique contributions to American society. Although many of the publications she submitted her essays to continued glorifying male cultural contributions, she was undeterred. Throughout the 1830s Beecher wrote and lectured publicly on her theories of moral instruction. She also published on other topics. In 1833, she and her sister, Harriet Beecher Stowe, produced a textbook on geography and Beecher wrote two works on religion. *Letters on the Difficulties of Religion* (1836) was a defense of Lyman Beecher in the wake of the "Lane Rebels'" exodus from the Lane Theological Seminary. *The Moral Instructor for Schools and Families: Containing Lessons on the Duties of Life, Arranged for Study and Recitation, Also Designed as a Reading Book for Schools* (1838) summarized her moral writings and encouraged all Americans to prioritize hard work. In these books, Beecher attempted to resolve the social tensions between religion, education, and economic differences, and offered suggestions on how children could be raised to embrace the democratic belief that hard work resulted in success, despite the reality that a solid work ethic did not always result in financial achievement.

Had Catharine Beecher been a man offering these social theories, she might have had an enthusiastic readership. As a woman, however, she was ridiculed, and her theories were nicknamed "Miss Beecher's difficulties."[3] But Beecher was nothing if not stubborn. Although she likely found the hostile reception to her writings frustrating, she remained determined to find an audience. Having spent more than a decade developing philosophies on religion, gender, and politics, she now compiled these theories into a domestic advice manual—a socially appropriate medium for a woman. In 1841, she published her *Treatise on Domestic Economy* and found her audience in middle-class white women. Her name would become synonymous with domesticity.

Treatise on Domestic Economy is best understood as having two sections, an explanation of American womanhood and instructions for the duties of womanhood. In the first, and shorter, section of the book Beecher reconciled gender inequality with the ideology of popular democracy and equal rights. She exaggerated the differences between the genders in order to exalt women's roles in the household, but she stressed women's intellectual equality with men. Basing her arguments on the observations of the French political scientist Alexis de Tocqueville, Beecher wrote that "It appears, then, that it is in America, alone, that women are raised to an equality with the other sex; and that, both in theory and practice, their interests are regarded as of equal value." She continued:

In civil and political affairs, American women take no interest or concern, except so far as they sympathize with their family and personal friends; but in all cases, in which they do feel concern, their opinions and feelings have a consideration, equal, or even superior, to that of the other sex.[4]

In other words, women's opinions were equal to men's, but women only chose to express them on occasion. Beecher emphasized women's agency and their choice to focus on their homes for the good of their families. In short, she assured women that they had *chosen* domesticity, it had not been thrust upon them.

The second section of *Treatise* was an instruction manual for caring for a home and family that insisted on the importance of women's domestic labor. This section was unique because Beecher did not presume that women knew how to be wives and mothers. There was no standardized text on household management prior to *Treatise*, it was simply assumed that women inherently knew how to cook, clean, and care for children. Catharine Beecher knew that this assumption was incorrect. For the first year after her mother's death, it was Catharine who cared for her younger siblings and cooked family meals. She only knew how because her mother had trained her. But what if she had been younger when her mother had died? Or her mother had not taught her domestic skills? She also understood that it was not just married women who maintained households. As a person who lived most of her adult life in the homes of relatives, Beecher knew that single women too were expected to maintain a home, even if it was for other people rather than themselves. Furthermore, as westward expansion increased many women found themselves far from female family members who might once have guided and advised them. Beecher wanted her book to be the resource that women in any of these positions turned to, and so *Treatise* was directed at a broad readership. It clearly explained in simple language how to run a home. Previous domestic guides had assumed that readers were already familiar with home management, but Beecher offered realistic suggestions on how to run a household. Her advice ranged from basic housekeeping—how to properly set a table, how to wash dishes, and how to get rid of bugs—to duties requiring more advanced skills—sewing a dress, decorating a parlor, and managing livestock. She even included diagrams for building a house.

Among the most useful chapters in *Treatise* was Beecher's overview of basic childcare. During the twentieth-century, parents often relied on Dr. Benjamin Spock's *The Common Sense Book of Baby and Child Care* or Heidi Murkoff's *What to Expect When You're Expecting* as guides for infant- and child-care. In the nineteenth-century, no such book existed until *Treatise* appeared. Using quotes from physicians, Beecher explained to her readers in detail how to care for an infant. In a typical passage, she advised her readers to "Dress the infant, so that it will be always warm, but not so as to cause perspiration."[5] She also instructed her readers on how to teach manners to children, ranging from how to address an adult to how to behave at the dinner table. Good manners, Beecher argued, were a display of the principles of democracy and benevolence.

Beecher also offered valuable advice on first aid. In the chapter "Accidents and Antidotes" she described how to deal with household mishaps such as choking, drowning, head injuries, and poisoning—all of which could be fatal without immediate medical care. During the nineteenth-century receiving treatment from a physician was a luxury that many people could not afford. Prior to the invention of the telephone doctors were summoned in person. This meant that travel must be paid for twice, first for the messenger's journey to alert the doctor to a family's need and second for the doctor's travel itself. In addition, there were fees for treatment. Even if a household could afford these expenses, there was no guarantee that the doctor would be found easily. Since physicians did not keep office hours, one might wait for hours for the doctor's return, be forced to leave and return later, or go in search of the doctor based on his last known location. In emergency cases this time delay could be deadly. The advent of paved roads and railroads linked to the Market Revolution remedied some of these difficulties because rural patients could more easily travel to town to see a physician and doctors could cover more territory. For many Americans, however, a physician's care remained impractical. Therefore, it was up to women as keepers of the home to administer to the sick, practicing what historians call domestic medicine.

Catharine Beecher was not the first to advocate domestic medicine. During the colonial and early republic periods, domestic medicine was based largely on herbal remedies passed down through female networks. By the nineteenth-century, medical advice manuals written by male physicians had also become the staple of most households. The authors of these manuals argued that most illnesses could be treated by ordinary people with medicines prepared from readily available ingredients. Like Beecher, these authors encouraged readers to adopt preventive measures including exercise, fresh air, and cleanliness. *Treatise* diverged from the typical medical guide, however, in its rejection of mainstream medicine, popularly known as heroic medicine.

Beecher's own ill health had made her suspicious of mainstream medical treatments. She believed they did more harm than good. She had good reason for her skepticism. For much of the nineteenth-century, doctors did not have to be licensed to practice medicine. This meant that many had been trained without medical school. Those who did attend college were not required to complete a medical residency, so it was not uncommon for physicians to set up their practices without ever having seen a baby born. The "heroic medicine" most practiced involved administering extreme treatments for disease including bloodletting, purging, and laxatives. It was believed that illness was caused by an imbalance in the body, and by regulating fluids one could restore health. Sadly, heroic medicine probably killed more people than it saved. Physicians now understand that germs, not unbalanced bodily fluids, lead to disease, but in Beecher's era, the scientific community was decades away from developing germ theory. Given these conditions—and the expense of calling a doctor—her instruction on home care was invaluable. *Treatise on Domestic Economy* was so widely read that Beecher's advice became standard domestic practice.

By 1843—only two years after its publication—*Treatise on Domestic Economy* had entered its fourth printing. It would be reprinted nearly every year until 1856, going through fifteen editions. At fifty cents (roughly $17 in modern currency) *Treatise* was affordable for most middle-class families.[6] Beecher's work also influenced other domestic authors, notably Sarah Josepha Hale, the editor of the popular woman's magazine *Godey's Lady's Book*. Whether Beecher was self-conscious about promoting a family life that she did not have is unclear. Her readership, however, was none the wiser. As Beecher's biographer Kathryn Kish Sklar noted,

> In the next three decades, Catharine Beecher could enter virtually any community in the United States and expect to be received as the heroine who had simplified and made understandable the mysterious arts of household maintenance, child rearing, gardening, cooking, cleaning, doctoring, and a dozen other responsibilities middle-class women assumed to keep their children and husbands alive and well.[7]

The mystery of what it took to be a "true woman" had finally been explained: within antebellum culture, *Treatise* served as an important manual for women who embraced their domestic roles but lacked the knowledge to run a home. *Treatise* was easy to understand, unlike other publications of the era, but its importance went beyond its readership and practical advice. Rather than positing a chasm between the separate spheres of men and women, Catharine Beecher insisted that women were part of society. Women's *choice* to focus their labor on the home allowed them to uphold American values, and in this created a unique mission for women. *Treatise* also established Beecher as an expert on all things domestic.

Although she was childless and remained unmarried, through her work she came to personify the ideal domestic woman. *Treatise on Domestic Economy* also made Catharine Beecher one of the most famous women of her time. Although she was also part of one of the most famous families, she had made her own name through writing and subsequent lectures. *Treatise* also provided her with financial stability, which she used together with her celebrity to promote her role as a leader in women's education.

Notes

1 Catharine Beecher, *The Elements of Mental and Moral Philosophy, Founded Upon Experience, Reason and the Bible* (Hartford:1831), 395.
2 C. Beecher, *Elements of Mental and Moral Philosophy*, 397.

3 Kathryn Kish Sklar, *Catharine Beecher: A Study in American Domesticity* (New York: W.W. Norton & Company, 1976), 129.
4 Catharine Beecher, *Treatise on Domestic Economy for the Use of Young Ladies at Home and at School* (New York: Harper & Brothers Publishers, 1849), 33.
5 C. Beecher, *Treatise*, 218.
6 C. Beecher, *Treatise*, 152.
7 Sklar, 152.

6
EDUCATION REFORM

Treatise on Domestic Economy gave Catharine Beecher a national stage for her philosophies. She was now firmly established as a domestic expert and could pursue her plans for the national system of female led education, she believed would further exalt women's social status. Despite her arguments for feminine authority, however, women were losing social power in the United States. As an organized woman's rights movement developed in response to this inferiority, Beecher struggled to find support for an educational plan that she believed would advance women's education.

Following the success of *Treatise on Domestic Economy*, Beecher divided her time between the Eastern and Western United States as she toured the country fundraising for western schools. *Treatise* had won her favor with wealthy Eastern families eager to support her career. She was also earning approximately $1,000 a year from *Treatise*, finally giving her financial stability. During the summer of 1843 Beecher lived in New York City but that winter she returned to Cincinnati where Lyman Beecher and several of her siblings still lived. She hoped that her connections in both New York and Ohio would further her educational plan for a national benevolent movement where the wealthy would pledge money to train teachers and establish schools in the West.

Beecher's first step in establishing her educational plan was to form an organization called the Central Committee for Promoting National Education. With the endorsement of her wealthy friends, the Committee was dedicated to educating women and recruiting them as teachers. She worried, however, that without a male leader the organization would lack the authority necessary for success. She asked her brother-in-law, Calvin Stowe, to head it. Stowe reluctantly took the position, but as a manager, he was exactly what she needed. His reputation as a minister provided credibility to the Central Committee, but he did not challenge Beecher's leadership. Throughout 1845, she lectured in Eastern cities on the importance of women's education in the West.

The campaign to raise money for western schools demonstrated Beecher's keen business sense. To promote her speaking engagements, she sent circulars signed by Calvin Stowe to local newspapers and ministers asking for the names of women who might be interested in pursuing teaching. She then held fundraising events for women's church groups, where she spoke about the desperate need for money to reform education.

In one of these lectures, entitled, *The Evils Suffered by American Women: The Causes and the Remedy*, Beecher played to her audiences' sympathies by first explaining the terrible conditions under which children were being educated. In New York State, the schools were so shabby, she said, that students were learning in buildings with "...unhung doors, broken sashes, absent panels, stilted benches, yawning roofs, and muddy, moldering floors."[1] They lacked comfortable seating. They had no playgrounds. The ventilation was inferior. These schools lacked proper outdoor toilets. And then there were the teachers who Beecher described as "low, vulgar, obscene, intemperate, and utterly incompetent to teach anything good."[2] In the West, she claimed, conditions were even worse. In Kentucky and Ohio, 200,000 children were uneducated for lack of schoolhouses and teachers. Something needed to be done for the future of the nation.

Beecher hoped that her movement to reform education would become a charity sponsored by women's organizations throughout the United States. She stressed the importance of the school room as an extension of the home, where women's moral influence would shape the minds of children. She even offered a solution to the problem of finding qualified teachers: look for them among working-class women. Catharine Beecher had often written about women as a homogenous group with middle-class interests. But now she appealed to her middle-class audience by describing the ways that working-class women's values and their physical health were at risk in wage-labor positions.

Beecher had herself seen the dangers to working women's physical and moral condition. While visiting the textile mills in Lowell, Massachusetts, she was appalled at the unhealthy conditions. Overwork and a lack of fresh air threatened the Mill Girls' health. Even more seriously, she argued, their moral wellbeing was also at risk. These young women visited theaters and dance halls after work. In boarding houses, men and women flirted with one another. Nineteenth-century religious doctrine forbade all these activities. For Beecher, the fact that these urban amusements attracted rural women to jobs in Lowell put the women's virtue at risk. She further worried that these girls would marry just to escape life in the mills. Beecher cautioned her readers against marrying for convenience. The circumstances in the mills, she argued, were exactly why women needed careers. There was no vocation more virtuous, she insisted, than teaching children.

The problem with using Lowell as an example, however, was that Catharine Beecher had portrayed women as victims who did not necessarily fit the description. In fact, the Lowell Mill Girls politicized their labor by organizing the first women's labor union during the 1830s. Throughout the 1840s—when Beecher would have visited—the textile factories relied primarily on these young American women from rural New England villages. Some of these women took factory work to supplement their parents' income. Others did so to pay for their brothers' college educations. But most women chose to pursue mill work to earn their own money before marriage. Their participation in the work force was temporary. Contrary to Beecher's belief that the factory workers were mistreated and would eagerly turn to careers in education if given the opportunity, many of these women saw their time in the mill as a temporary experience before marriage and motherhood. Within the next decade, however, the conditions of the Lowell Mills deteriorated as native-born workers were replaced with cheaper Irish immigrant labor. Financially dependent on this factory work, these immigrant women would have also been unlikely to leave their positions to pursue teaching.

Beecher's argument was not specifically intended to lure the Mill Girls away from the factories. It was directed at the wealthy women she hoped would donate to her Central Committee for Promoting National Education. Her lecture's central message was to them. She explained to her wealthy audience that it was their duty, as the sex with the "superior character," to ensure that both working-class women and children were cared for. "It is the immediate object of this enterprise now presented," Beecher explained,

> to engage American women to assert the great power and influence put into their hands, the remedy the evils which now oppress their countrywoman, and thus, at the same time, and by the same method, to secure a proper education to the vast multitude of neglected American children all over the land.[3]

Her plan, she explained, was for the Central Committee for Promoting National Education to appoint a male board of managers to oversee fundraising activities conducted by local women. The funds would then be used to pay for schools and for new teachers' salaries. She also cleverly encouraged her audiences to purchase *Treatise on Domestic Economy* as well as her follow up publication, *Domestic Receipt Book*—a collection of recipes—because half of the profits would be donated to training programs. Although Beecher misrepresented the ways that the profits would be distributed between herself, her publisher, and the charity, the promotion of her books as part of a larger cause also revealed that she was a skilled self-publicist.

Beecher's fundraising speeches were covered extensively in local newspapers. Through them, she raised thousands of dollars for her committee. She soon had the endorsement of male educational reformers, including Horace Mann, whose support further legitimatized her work. By 1846, she had raised enough money to pay a full-time agent to run her committee. Calvin Stowe was relieved of his duties and Beecher hired the governor of Vermont, William Slade, who had contacted her about the position. Slade's main job was to locate communities in the West that were interested in hiring the teachers Beecher recruited in the East.

Catharine Beecher's success in fundraising for western schools coincided with the professionalization of teaching. This development was part of a successful movement in many states to create a public elementary (or common) school system. Common schools were supported by the state through taxes and were, as their name suggests, developed according to standards that were adapted throughout the state. Their proponents (of whom Horace Mann was the most famous) argued that common schools would help instill patriotic values in their students, preparing them to be virtuous and responsible citizens. The common school movement also involved the establishment of normal schools, or teacher-training academies, in order to provide the vastly expanded need for staff for these primary schools. This development occurred while industrial and clerical job sectors were also expanding. These sectors became dominated by men, leaving single women to fill the ranks of teaching. By 1860, three-quarters of American teachers were women. Teaching came to be seen, as Beecher put it, as "a *profession*, offering influence, respectability, and independence" without violating "the prescribed boundaries of feminine modesty."[4] Teaching was becoming a career associated with women.

To one extent the increase in female teachers demonstrates that Beecher's stance on women as naturally suited to teaching was embraced by society at large. For most state legislators, however, the preference for female teachers was a dollars-and-cents issue; women could be hired at lower salaries than men. Many of these politicians believed that men were the most competent teachers, but if the large influx of immigrants and western migrants increased the needs for schools, staffing them with women teachers would not increase the tax base. It was argued that because women did not have to financially support a family and would only be working until they married, the lower salaries made sense.

Beecher overlooked this last point in her fundraising speeches, and she never spoke of money as she encouraged women to pursue teaching. Instead, she focused her lectures on her philosophy of education. One of her goals was to ensure that Moral Training and Domestic Economy were taught in all women's high schools. And, because she saw that the classroom as analogous to the home, it was not only women's domain, but also a place where childless women could embrace the role of mother. By linking the home to school, and mother to teacher, Beecher was using the older tenets of Republican Motherhood to provide women with a civic duty. The argument, that it was women's obligation to confront national immoralities by educating children, had been made during the eighteenth-century. It was also made by women of Beecher's own generation, including Angelina Grimke. Unlike many of her contemporaries, however, Beecher argued that women's value to society could be demonstrated without any active political participation. Just as she had done in her 1837 debate with Angelina Grimke, she declared that the political sphere was not for women Not surprisingly, when the Woman's Rights Movement was officially founded in 1848, Beecher opposed it.

The formation of an organized women's rights movement was the culmination of decades of discussions about white women's roles as citizens. Republican Motherhood offered one solution, but many women of Catharine Beecher's generation also aspired to public roles. Social reform offered this opportunity. During the Second Great Awakening, middle- and upper-class women were encouraged to perform charity work to help the less fortunate. While the concept of separate spheres was also developing, some women were able to make public aid their careers since it was viewed as an extension of their roles as wives and mothers. Women were encouraged to visit the sick, promote church attendance, support temperance, and endorse legislation favored by their husbands. Some women fundraised for orphanages or provided aid to the poor. Other women ran businesses in the name of benevolence. These women were able to manipulate the language of true womanhood to participate in the public sphere. They could also use charity work to distinguish their middle-class status from the status of the poorer classes they were aiding. An important offshoot of this charity work was female abolitionism.

While female abolitionists were a minority within national organizations, there were several examples of women who became famous for their antislavery activism. For example, abolitionist Abby Kelley began her career with the Lynn Female Antislavery Society, but by the late 1830s, she had begun traveling with William Lloyd Garrison and his colleagues giving speeches calling for the immediate abolition of slavery. In 1838 she famously gave an antislavery speech to a mixed audience of men and women—something considered scandalous at the time. Sarah and Angelina Grimke also spoke to large mixed audiences about their experiences as the daughters of a slaveowner. Lucretia Mott was known for her powerful orations and co-founded the Philadelphia Female Anti-Slavery Society in 1833. Amy Kirby Post hosted antislavery lectures in her home and co-founded the Western Anti-Slavery Society in 1842.

These undertakings did not come without a personal price, however. Many female reformers chose to remain single. Angelina Grimke's public career ended following her 1838 marriage to abolitionist Theodore Weld. In 1845 Amy Kirby Post withdrew from Quakerism after ministers condemned the methods of radical antislavery reformers. Nevertheless, this generation of social reformers would mentor the most famous generation of white female abolitionists including Lucy Stone, Elizabeth Cady Stanton, and Susan B. Anthony.

African American women too were able to establish careers within the antislavery movement. Maria W. Stewart was the first American woman to speak publicly before an audience of men and women in 1832. Sarah Mapp Douglass was a contributor to antislavery newspapers including *The Liberator* and educated the free Black community in New York and Philadelphia. Charlotte Forten and her daughters Sarah, Margaretta and Harriet (who were on the committee to form the Philadelphia Anti-Slavery Society along with Lucretia Mott), and granddaughter Charlotte L. publicly lectured and published articles on abolition. They also aided runaway slaves. During the Civil War Charlotte L. Forten (later Grimke when she married the nephew of Sarah and Angelina Grimke) was the first African American teacher to travel to the South Carolina Sea Islands to teach formerly enslaved children. Perhaps the most famous African American female abolitionists were Sojourner Truth and Harriet Tubman. Truth lectured extensively on abolition and women's rights. Tubman became a legend within the antislavery movement for her work on the Underground Railroad and as a Union spy during the Civil War.

Yet despite women's success in promoting antislavery principles, they did not enter the ranks of organizational leadership. Certain abolitionist societies actually banned women from leadership positions, while in other women were excluded from meetings. For example, in 1840, when abolitionists Lucretia Mott and Elizabeth Cady Stanton attended the World's Anti-Slavery Convention in London, they were turned away at the door because of their gender. Mott had been selected as one of seven female delegates to the World's Convention, but officials in London refused to budge on their no female policy. Eventually, the women negotiated sitting in the balcony on the condition that they did not speak during the meeting.

The snub in London was particularly demonstrative of gender biases within the antislavery movement. Fifty-five-year-old Lucretia Mott was a highly respected Quaker Minister, a veteran abolitionist, and the leader of Philadelphia's women's abolitionist movement. Twenty-five-year-old Elizabeth Cady Stanton was less experienced, but her familial ties—Stanton's father was the New York Supreme Court Judge Daniel Cady, her cousin the abolitionist Gerrit Smith, and her husband Henry Stanton, an antislavery writer and orator—combined with her knowledge of the law and passion for social reform made her a promising abolitionist. London was the first time that Mott and Stanton met, but their experience at the World Abolitionist Society and their shared beliefs in reform and women's rights united the two. When they returned to the United States, Stanton and Mott began discussing the creation of a women's rights movement. Eight years later, in 1848, Mott, Stanton, and activists Mary M'Clintock, Martha Coffin Wright, and Jane Hunt organized the first woman's rights convention in Seneca Falls, New York.

The Seneca Falls Convention is often used by historians as the starting point for the organized woman's rights movement (reformers chose the word "woman" over the grammatically correct "women" to show unity). However, this is a simplification of women's history. The demand for women's equality was not a new subject for convention attendees. The issue had been debated in newspaper articles by ministers, educators, politicians, and social reformers for decades. During the eighteenth century, intellectuals like Judith Sargent Murray and Susannah Rowson had argued for women's natural equality to men. In 1834 the mill workers in Lowell organized to protest wage cuts and during the 1840s they formed the Female Labor Reform Association to campaign for a ten-hour workday. In 1837 Oberlin College in Ohio was the first college in America to admit women as well as men, Black or White. One year later, abolitionist Sarah Grimke published *Letters on the Equality of the Sexes* in which she challenged the idea that men were naturally superior to women. Seneca Falls, however, was the first organized effort to discuss the issue. Three hundred women and men attended the Seneca Falls Convention. It was during this meeting that the Declaration of Sentiments, a manifesto calling for broad reforms to ensure female equality, was first read. The founders of the Seneca Falls Convention modeled this declaration on the Declaration of Independence. Like the Founding Fathers, the authors of the Declaration of Sentiments outlined their grievances and proposed their solutions. The Declaration demanded the right of women to own property, to obtain a divorce, to enjoy equal access to jobs, and education. It also called for the right to vote. In total, sixty-eight women and thirty-two men signed the Declaration of Sentiments.

Catharine Beecher shared many of the goals of the Seneca Falls feminists. Like these radical women, she supported equal educational opportunities for women and access to better paying jobs. But, although she had personally suffered many of the frustrations addressed by the Declaration of Sentiments, she refused to join the Woman's Rights Movement. For Beecher was fundamentally at odds with the movement's basic premise: that the sexes were equal in all regards. As a traditionalist, she believed that the Bible had enjoyed women to submit to men's will. But the Bible had also instructed men to treat women as their "superiors in value and dignity, and protect their interest *more* than their own."[5] Thus, women did not need political rights; they could achieve all their goals by influencing lawmakers, "*in an acceptable manner.*"[6] Women's power, she was arguing, lay in their innate differences from men, not in their similarities. The path women should take was clear:

> Instead of rushing into the political arena to join in the scramble for office, or attempting to wedge into the overcrowded learned professions of men, let woman raise and dignify her own profession, and endow posts of honor and emolument in it, that are suited to the characters and duties of her sex.[7]

The Woman's Rights Movement was intended to push women outside of their sphere instead of elevating it. Beecher would not endorse this

Besides, Beecher had no time to take on another project. Her education plan had become more complicated than she anticipated. By 1847, it appeared that her goal of sending teachers to the West was achieved. Governor Slade had proven to be an effective manager and within the next ten years, the Committee for Promoting National Education would place over 400 teachers in schools. Yet Slade's efficiency created problems for Beecher. She was no longer needed to recruit teachers. Instead, her job collecting donations and scheduling training for new teachers effectively made her a secretary. Beecher was displeased. She wanted to remain in control of every element of the organization. Slade too was disillusioned with the work, and began to use his authority as manager to revise Beecher's original plans. For example, Beecher had arranged for the home base of the Central Committee to be Cincinnati, where she assured Slade there was strong local support for the organization's mission. When Slade arrived, however, he found that the community leaders were opposed to the organization. Slade left Cincinnati after only three months, and established Cleveland as the new base for the Central Committee. Here, he renamed the organization the National Board of Popular Education. Slade and the Board then cut the emergency funds set aside for teachers once they arrived in their new communities. Beecher was not consulted on any of these decisions. This left her at a crossroad: should she accept Slade's leadership, or break with the National Board of Popular Education?

Beecher's dilemma also reflected a crisis of self. At age 47, her life was a series of contradictions. Through her writing she had helped created a culture of domesticity and had become an expert on domestic economy, yet she had no home of her own. She advised women on childcare, but was not a mother. She recruited teachers, but she had left that profession. Now, she found herself undermined by the man she had hired to run her organization. Beecher was not alone in her frustrations. Historians have noted that during the 1840s, American women were becoming increasingly aware of their loss in social and economic status and in their influence in society. As the vote expanded to include more White men, including immigrants, women's status and influence had diminished. The frustrations felt by many had played a significant role in creating the Seneca Falls Convention. Social reform movements had proved one outlet for women to express their political views, but not all women saw political activism as the solution. Some simply felt helpless. As women saw their world narrowing, they often suffered mental distress, which was frequently diagnosed as female hysteria.

During the nineteenth-century, female hysteria was believed to be a neurological disorder that could cause everything from infertility to fainting or anxiety. In fact, almost all physical or mental ailments could be diagnosed as hysteria. In some situations, this diagnosis reflected the limitations of medical knowledge. Women suffering from post-partem depression, post-traumatic stress disorder, or major depressive disorder, were typically diagnosed with hysteria. In other situations, the thoughts and feelings of women who challenged the status quo were dismissed as symptoms of hysteria. Some women, however, used their diagnosis of hysteria to take a break from the rigors of daily life. Catharine Beecher was one. For Beecher, her repeated nervous breakdowns were a way of coping with stress, and a socially acceptable way to retreat from public life for periods of time. The summer of 1847 was one of those times. Overwhelmed by her frustrations with Governor Slade, Catharine Beecher chose to recuperate at one of her favorite spas, a water cure facility in Battleboro, Vermont.

Catharine Beecher's choice of this Vermont spa reflected the influence water cure, a fringe health movement, had on her and many social reformers of the nineteenth-century. The movement had originated in Germany in 1816, and was based on the premise that the body could be cured of any disorder by the external and internal use of water. These principles were brought to the United States during the 1840s by physicians who were skeptical of heroic medicine. In an era when Americans bathed infrequently, and diseases like cholera were caused by drinking unclean water, water was not part of daily life. Water cure physicians encouraged patients to bathe and drink eight glasses of natural spring water daily. They also encouraged patients to exercise regularly, to wear loose clothing, and to be careful about their diets and drinking habits. Beecher had promoted all these suggestions in *A Treatise on Domestic Economy*. While modern standards would include these health practices, water cure spas also promoted other more unusual treatments. The sitz bath, for example, involved sitting in a tepid tub of water with the feet hanging out. During a wet sheet pack treatment, a patient was wrapped in a cold, wet sheet, and then covered with four blankets. Catharine Beecher experienced both. These treatments were aimed at increasing circulation and were supposed to heal everything from a cold to a tumor.

For middle-class women, however, water cure spas were not only places of healing, but also spaces to recover from the laborious tasks of wifedom and motherhood. After visiting one such spa, Isabella Beecher Hooker wrote to her husband, "It is such a relief—to have nobody to care for—nothing that *must* be done."[8] She was not alone in her desire for a break. Although rejected by mainstream medical professionals, water cure treatments had a loyal following. In 1849, there were thirty water cure facilities in nine states; soon there would be 200 spas between Maine and San Francisco. Throughout the 1840s and 1850s, the mental health issues from which Catharine Beecher had suffered in her early 30s escalated; she visited no fewer than thirteen water cure facilities. For Beecher, water cure was a respite from her anxieties and stresses, and she recommended other women partake. During the summer of 1847 she invited two friends, Delia Bacon and Nany Johnson, to join her at Battleboro.

Beecher's close friendships reflected a common nineteenth-century social pattern. For many women these female friendships were among their most intimate relationships. While some of these relationships evolved romantically, for many women same-sex friendships filled the void left by unhappy marriages or the absence of any husband at all. This was the case for Catharine Beecher, but her relationship with these two particular young women went beyond simply common interests; she saw in each woman an element of herself.

Perhaps Beecher's most dramatic of the two relationships was with writer Delia Bacon. Bacon had been one of Beecher's students at Hartford during the 1820s. Catharine Beecher and Delia Bacon had much in common. They both came from families of ministers. Both had careers as writers. Neither had married. During that spring of 1847 Bacon was also recovering from a personal scandal, and so when her former teacher, Catharine Beecher, invited her to Battleboro, she accepted.

Beecher was aware of Bacon's personal troubles when she extended the invitation. In fact, Beecher had found herself in the middle of Bacon's scandal. While living in a boarding house in New Haven, Connecticut, Bacon, then in her mid-30s, had engaged in a flirtation with a 23-year-old minister, Alexander McWhorter. A year into this relationship, Catharine Beecher asked a mutual friend if Bacon and McWhorter were engaged. It was uncommon for two unmarried people to spend so much time together without a commitment. When confronted with the status of their relationship, however, McWhorter denied there was one. Instead, McWhorter claimed Bacon had pursued him, which was inappropriate for women according to nineteenth-century standards of decorum. Bacon defended herself, claiming that McWhorter had indeed proposed to her. Intent on defending his sister's honor, Bacon's brother charged McWhorter with the Christian sins of slander, lying, and disgraceful conduct. In addition to damaging Delia Bacon's personal reputation, her family worried that her career as a writer would be affected. While McWhorter had not broken any civil laws, as a minister these were serious charges. The case was tried before an ecclesiastical, or Christian, court of ministers.

Catharine Beecher was Delia Bacon's constant companion during the trial. She sat with Bacon eight hours a day for two weeks while friends and acquaintances testified. Beecher was also a witness on her friend's behalf. For Bacon, this period of her life was characterized by "utter helplessness, human despair, [and] sorrow..."[9] All she wanted was her reputation restored. Beecher, however, treated Bacon as a martyr. For Beecher, the trial triggered old resentments against the clerical elite. She remembered how her father had tried to force her into conversion following Alexander Fischer's death. She was also enraged by the hypocrisy of a society that pushed women to marry but condemned them if they pursued a man. Instead, women were supposed to play games, pretending they were not interested in men. "By the constitution of nature, by the ordinance of Providence, by the training of family and school, by the influence of society, and by the whole current of poetry and literature," Beecher wrote,

> woman is educated to feel that a happy marriage is the summit of all earthly felicity. And yet, by a fantasy of custom, it has become one of the most disgraceful of all acts for a woman to acknowledge that she is seeking this felicity.[10]

Women, she implied, were in a no-win situation.

Beecher's anger only intensified when the ecclesiastical court voted to acquit Alexander McWhorter. He was reprimanded for "imprudence," or carelessness, but avoided any other consequences. It was Delia Bacon whose reputation was ruined. In the summer of 1847 Beecher took Bacon to Battleboro to recover from the stress of the trial. One can imagine the two taking daily walks and relaxing in baths, as was customary at water cure facilities. Perhaps they bonded over the tension caused by the trial. Whatever their relationship was that summer, however, it would not last. While the two remained friends for a few more years and even stayed at other water cure institutions together, Beecher's growing desperation to save Bacon's reputation would end their friendship.

In 1850 Catharine Beecher published a book entitled, *Truth Stranger than Fiction*, detailing Bacon's relationship with Alexander McWhorter and the subsequent trial. Delia Bacon begged her not to publish the book, telling her "I am tired of being a victim!" But Beecher was certain that her book would validate Bacon's experiences. "I did not expect to obtain your consent, and I do not wish for your help," she told Delia Bacon, "I know I can convince you that your attempting such opposition would be turning traitor to the very principles for which you have suffered so bitterly, yet so bravely."[11] The book was published in 1850, and Beecher hoped that with her reputation restored, Delia Bacon might teach in one of the western schools she had founded. But Bacon's distress over the book was sincere, and shortly after the publication of *Truth Stranger than Fiction*, she moved to England, where she lived until shortly before her death in 1859. Beecher was obviously fond of Bacon. She once described her as possessing "the embryo of rare gifts of eloquence in thought and expression, and she was pre-eminently one who would be pointed out as genius…" Yet she disregarded her friend's feelings to advance her own agenda. Beecher, ever the self-promoter, sent copies of *Truth Stranger than Fiction* to congregations throughout New England, religious journals, and the ladies committees that supported her educational mission. She wanted as many people as possible to read the account of clerical misconduct. As one historian noted, "Catharine's public and personal experience had become so intermingled that she could not distinguish between them."[12] Delia Bacon's story had become a way for Beecher to challenge the authority of Christian ministers and advance her definition of social morality. In the process she never doubted she had Delia Bacon's best interests at heart, even if her actions cost her the friendship.

Beecher's second significant female friendship during the summer of 1847 was with a young teacher named Nancy Johnson. Johnson had been recommended by Governor Slade to work as Beecher's secretary and Catharine subsequently invited Johnson to join her at Battleboro. Beecher must have found Nancy Johnson a welcome distraction from Delia Bacon for the two began planning on a western campaign to raise money for the schools. Over the course of several months, Beecher's relationship with Nancy Johnson deepened into one of mentor and friend.

Like Beecher, Nancy Johnson was a teacher, but more from necessity than choice. A childhood accident had led to one of Johnson's feet being amputated, a disability that she believed made her unmarriageable. Teaching was the most obvious route for a woman who would not marry. Beecher sympathized with Johnson's plight. She often described herself as an invalid because of her frequent illnesses, that at times included the paralysis of a hand and foot. For Beecher, invalidism seems to have been part of her identity, probably because it gave her a socially acceptable excuse to step away from her regular responsibilities. But paradoxically, that invalidism was empowering. By seeking treatment at water cure facilities, Beecher was able to assert autonomy over her own health, and when she recruited other women to water cure, she was demonstrating that, although she may be ill, she was still useful. This was important since disability was heavily stigmatized during this era, and it could place a heavy burden on an individual or family. Social security disability benefits would not be implemented until the twentieth century, and this meant that individuals who could not physically care for or financially support themselves became entirely dependent on their families. When they had no one to care for them, the disabled were institutionalized. Nancy Johnson's training as a teacher had prepared her for a career and correspondence indicates that her family was loving and supportive, yet she may still have felt intense pressure to prove her worth. She was thrilled when none of the other patients at Battlebroro noticed her prosthetic foot. "Nobody here *guesses* that I am *lame*," she wrote her father.[13] Among the patients only Catharine Beecher knew, and she had promised Johnson not to divulge her secret.

Throughout the spring of 1847, the friendship between these two invalids deepened. Beecher encouraged Johnson to dedicate herself to water cure, and Johnson's letters home were filled with Catharine Beecher's advice. The following winter, Beecher invited Johnson to come on a fundraising tour of Philadelphia, Baltimore, Washington, and Cincinnati. Johnson accepted. It was clear that the young woman was enamored with Beecher, and flattered by her attention. Writing to her father she reported that "[Catharine Beecher] took a great fancy to me and [that she] is my true friend is certainly true. I love her too and having been with her I know that she is, always kind and considerate."[14] But this trip was more than simply a way to raise money.

Each of these two women had personal motives for the trip. For Beecher, this western tour would serve as a litmus test of whether Governor Slade still played a necessary role in accomplishing her educational mission, and she was also searching for a new location to open a school. For Nancy Johnson, the trip was an adventure, but it also promised to aid her career. "I should see much of the world and be introduced to the very best society, religious and literary, that these cities offer," she told her family.[15] But Johnson also hoped her connection to Catharine Beecher would help her find employment. She had been unable to secure a teaching position after her stay at Battleboro but noted:

I always find that to have been with [Catharine Beecher] is enough to recommend me to the attention of all the great and good and to be her intimate friend is as high a compliment as could be paid me.[16]

For Johnson, this trip must have seemed like a once in a lifetime opportunity. In February 1848 Johnson and Beecher met in Philadelphia and began their journey.

Everywhere they went Beecher's name drew crowds of women eager to hear an expert on domesticity and education speak. She told her audiences that money was needed to improve western schools and she read aloud letters from desperate teachers describing schoolhouses without windows, illiterate townspeople, and the lack of money to purchase books. She described one teacher who became so ill after arriving at her post that she had to give up her job. She laid the blame for these predicaments on Governor Slade and confided to her audience that he had failed his duty to these teachers by refusing to provide for them after their arrival in new communities. The crowds must have moved by Beecher's concern because she raised several hundred dollars in the first two cities. With this money Beecher and Johnson were able to travel West, where they continued fundraising and searching for the ideal community to establish Beecher's new seminary. This school would adhere to a new type of educational structure of Catharine's own design, that she called college plan.

Catharine Beecher had been developing the college plan since she worked at the Hartford Female Seminary. Its premise was that teachers at women's schools should enjoy the same prestige and receive the same respect and job security as professors at male colleges. As Beecher saw it, female educators' power was limited by the hierarchy that placed the principal—usually a man—above teachers. She also insisted that students' tuition be used to pay teachers' salaries rather than fund an unreliable endowment. The cooperative atmosphere she advocated placed the responsibility of running the school on everyone, rather than on a single administrator. In her view, her teachers were critical to American society because they prepared women to pursue their "true profession": homemaker and educator of the next generation. She simply needed to find a community receptive to the college plan. As she and Nancy Johnson traveled West, Beecher identified two such communities, Burlington, Iowa, and Quincy, Illinois.

According to Beecher, the citizens of Burlington and Quincy were so eager to support female seminaries that they made generous offers while she and Johnson were still scouting. Beecher accepted and immediately assigned teachers to the schools. In early summer 1848, Beecher and Johnson traveled to Burlington, Iowa to oversee the opening of the seminary there. But when they arrived, they found that no preparations had been made. A disappointed Beecher took on the role of locating and renting a building. She spent $300 of her own money on furniture. She also hired two teachers and took on the job of principal, herself. Johnson also began teaching there. But the work was more than Beecher was prepared for, and her already tense relationship with Governor Slade was becoming more strained. When she wrote to him asking that he send at least two more teachers, no teachers ever arrived. Catharine, already mentally fragile, took this as a personal attack by Slade. Another episode of mental and physical illness followed. After spending weeks in bed, Beecher finally decided to return East. She was so weak that she had to be carried from her bed to the boat transporting her. Beecher spent the next several months at a water cure facility while Nancy Johnson was left in charge of the Burlington school. In Beecher's absence, the situation in Burlington grew worse. Johnson had been left with little money or staff to run the school. She was one of three teachers, but was also burdened with every essential task from cooking and cleaning to bookkeeping. The school's finances were so desperate that Johnson had to bargain for basic supplies such as wood, coal, flour, and meat, noting "Oh, it required a heap of *knowledge* and *dignity* and *versatility*."[17] Johnson also repeatedly wrote to the National Board of Popular Education asking for more money. When none arrived, she closed the school and went to St. Louis to stay with relatives. The school had only been open for seven months. The Quincy school would also eventually fail in Beecher's absence. When Beecher finally recovered in the spring of 1849 Johnson had already decided to return home to Vermont.

Beecher's relationship with Nancy Johnson followed a pattern common with her female friendships. As with Delia Bacon, Beecher had begun her relationship with Johnson as a mentor. She looked for women that reminded her of herself and pushed them to excel. But in both her friendships with Bacon and Johnson, Beecher was opportunistic. She may not have originally intended to use her friendships for personal gain, but neither did she retreat from taking advantage when the opportunity arose. Her insecurity about the limitations of her gender and her desire to challenge male authority often proved too much for her delicate nervous system. When that happened, Beecher either abandoned a project, or pushed it onto someone else. In the case of Burlington, Iowa, that person was Nancy Johnson, who was left to manage a frontier school alone and with little support. Beecher seemed to have turned her back on the school. When Johnson had decided to leave the Midwest for Vermont in 1849, Beecher did not try to dissuade her. She too had moved on.

Shortly after the Iowa and Illinois schools failed, Catharine Beecher severed ties with the Board of National Popular Education. She blamed Governor Slade for the schools' closures because he failed to send the teachers she had requested. It was not his reputation at risk, she fumed, but her own. Beecher worried that she could no longer find support for the college plan if "it was regarded by the public, and by all concerned in the affair, as an exhibition of the inexpediency of the *new* method proposed."[18] Slade was no fonder of Catharine Beecher at this point than she was of him. When Beecher learned that Slade had told people that neither he nor the Board believed she would be able to raise enough money to support her impractical educational plan, Beecher declared that "…

the agency which I had labored so long to establish, became the main embarrassment in carrying out the enterprise for which it was instituted."[19] Beecher's next school venture would be undertaken on her own. She had located a new site for a female seminary and had a new co-teacher. Catharine Beecher was moving to Milwaukee, Wisconsin.

Notes

1 Catharine Beecher, *The Evils Suffered by American Women and American Children: The Causes and Remedy* (New York: Harper and Brothers, 1847), 4.
2 C. Beecher, *The Evils Suffered by American Women and American Children*, 4.
3 C. Beecher, *The Evils Suffered by American Women and American Children*, 12.
4 Milton Rugoff, *The Beechers: An American Family in the Nineteenth-Century* (New York: Harper & Row Publishers, 1981), 61.
5 Catharine Beecher, *The True Remedy for the Wrongs of Woman: With a History of An Enterprise Having that for Its Object* (Boston: Philips, Sampson & Co., 1851), 229.
6 C. Beecher, *The True Remedy for the Wrongs of Woman*, 231.
7 C. Beecher, *The True Remedy for the Wrongs of Woman*, 232.
8 Barbara A. White, *The Beecher Sisters* (New Haven: Yale University Press, 2003), 77.
9 Catharine Beecher, *Truth Stranger Than Fiction: A Narrative of Recent Transactions, Involving Enquiries in Regard to the Principles of Honor, Truth, and Justice, Which Obtain in a Distinguished American University* (Boston: Phillips, Sampson & Co., 1850), 259.
10 C. Beecher, *Truth Stranger Than Fiction*, 9.
11 C. Beecher, *Truth Stranger Than Fiction*, 277.
12 Kathryn Kish Sklar, *Catharine Beecher: A Study in American Domesticity* (New York: W.W. Norton & Company, 1976), 192.
13 Nancy Johnson to David Johnson, March 13–15, 1847, Johnson Family Papers Ms 100587, Connecticut Historical Society.
14 Nancy Johnson to David Johnson, June 22, 1848.
15 Ibid.
16 Ibid.
17 Nancy Johnson to David Johnson, September 20, 1848.
18 C. Beecher, *The True Remedy for the Wrongs of Woman*, 128.
19 C. Beecher, *The True Remedy for the Wrongs of Woman*, 139.

7
THE PROFESSIONALIZATION OF WOMANHOOD

Wisconsin was still the frontier in 1850 when Catharine Beecher began promoting her Milwaukee Female Seminary. The state was only two years old, and Milwaukee a scant twenty years old. With only 20,000 residents, Milwaukee was home to a combination of self-taught businessmen, eastern transplants, and immigrants whose competition for elite class status created social tension. The businessmen mimicked the traditions of the Eastern elite, only to have their inadequacies exposed by new settlers. Wealthier frontier people attempted to maintain their social status by sending their daughters to eastern schools, but this proved to be expensive and did little to prepare these young women for life in a frontier city. The simplest solution was for Milwaukee to establish its own school, one that would uphold eastern standards of female education. And for this, community leaders contacted Catharine Beecher. Beecher's time in Milwaukee would coincide with a personal shift in her educational goals. She no longer portrayed women as the saviors of the nation. Instead, she insisted that women's domestic roles should be seen as professional positions.

It was Lucy Parsons, an advocate of female education who had peaked Beecher's interest in Milwaukee. Parsons had founded a school in Milwaukee in 1848. She wanted Beecher to collaborate with her in re-organizing the school according to Beecher's pedagogical principles. If she would implement her college plan, Parsons pledged to teach in the new school. Beecher had only recently recovered from her illness following the failure of the Burlington school, but she visited Milwaukee. She was impressed. As she had with her other schools, Beecher promised to provide teachers if the townspeople would secure a building. She also volunteered to fund a library. It was agreed that the community would elect the school's board of trustees. With these terms agreed upon,

DOI: 10.4324/b23305-8

Beecher began organizing a women's school in Milwaukee. To help her in this venture, Beecher recruited Mary Mortimer, a teacher she had met in her travels.

Mary Mortimer was an experienced teacher by the time that she met Catharine Beecher in 1849. Beecher may have been drawn to Mortimer (as she had been to Nancy Johnson) because Mortimer was a fellow invalid. She suffered from recurring paralysis in her right hand and foot, just as Beecher did. Initially, when Beecher asked Mortimer to be the "leading spirit" in the school she was founding, Mortimer refused, citing ill health. Beecher, ever dictatorial, demanded to know details.[1] As Mary Mortimer recounted to friends:

> [Beecher] closed [her letter] with a wish for a full history of my ailments, and expressed a hope of being able to take me to a Water Cure Establishment, She [sic] said nothing about time, except that in a fortnight I should receive definite word as to '*time, place* and *(sic) plan.*' One week afterward, instead of two, came a second letter, wishing me to set off *immediately* for [the Round Hill Water-Cure].

Mortimer feared that "it would be treating [Beecher] ungenerously to refuse to come." So, she set off from New York to the Round Hill Water-Cure in Massachusetts. Beecher met Mortimer upon her arrival and immediately advised that as part of her treatment she stop writing letters. "I must obey," Mortimer wrote to her friends, but her tone was jovial.[2] Six weeks later, she wrote that Beecher had arranged for her to transfer to another water cure institution. "Miss Beecher has been so kind, so benevolent so thoughtful..." Mortimer told friends.[3] Meanwhile, Beecher had been fundraising throughout the East for the Milwaukee Female Institute. By 1850, Mary Mortimer along with Lucy Parsons and two other women had all signed on to teach at the Milwaukee Female Institute and Beecher had raised twenty-three hundred dollars for the school. It was now up to the local citizens to rent a temporary schoolhouse while they erected a permanent building. Beecher also hoped that Milwaukee would be a place where she could retire.

Beecher's desire to make Milwaukee her permanent home likely reflected her emotional state rather than a particular fondness for Wisconsin. 1849 had been a year of change and disappointment. Her friendships with Delia Bacon and Nancy Johnson were ending. The college plan in Iowa had been a disaster, and Beecher had severed ties with Governor Slade and the National Board of Popular Education. The Milwaukee Female Institute made her hopeful, however. She noted that "she had never saw a school that improved more in every valuable respect. Such intelligent, willing, and docile pupils, such capable and amiable associates, and such kind, competent, and efficient trustees have seldom been so happily united."[4] It seemed like a fresh start.

In Milwaukee Beecher was also able to practice the domestic skills that she so valued. For the first two months that the Milwaukee Female Institute was in operation, Beecher found it necessary, on account of my health and that of the other ladies, to go to housekeeping in the school building. In doing this, I had the whole responsibility of making all the purchases, and directing every detail, just as every housekeeper does in going to housekeeping, and for those two months I had the same family care as other housekeepers have.[5]

Beecher made sure that every room was comfortable, from each teacher's living space to the school rooms that she wanted carpeted. Flowers were to be planted in the yard. With these preparations under way, Beecher implemented the next phase of her plan: "[prove] that the sale of books can be made an efficient mode for sustaining educational agencies."[6] Toward this end, she returned to Hartford, where she wrote a book, *True Remedy for the Wrongs of Women*, that promoted her new educational plan and the Milwaukee Female Institute.

Published in 1851, *True Remedy for the Wrongs of Women* explained three tenets of Beecher's educational agenda. First, women's colleges should be founded in urban areas where women would have the most influence. Next, the faculty of women's colleges should have responsibility equal to the principal's. Last, Beecher emphasized that the purpose of women's colleges was to prepare the students for their "true professions" as teachers and homemakers. Therefore, each school should have a normal department and a department of domestic economy, just as the Milwaukee Female Institute would. These goals were also in line with Beecher's personal needs. She was a social person, and did best when she lived in urban centers where she could maintain an active social life. She also wanted to provide acceptable career options for other single women, options that would give them the same prestige as matrimony. Finally, the Department of Domestic Economy was her passion project. When the Milwaukee Female Institute opened, Beecher happily let Mary Mortimer take over the normal department so that she could oversee teaching domestic economy. The Milwaukee Female Institute, she anticipated, would become the model for other women's schools. It also became imperative for Beecher that Milwaukee become her permanent home.

Beecher's willingness to embrace domesticity on behalf of the Milwaukee teachers revealed her desire to have her own home. She had spent her adult life living with family members and in boarding houses. By 1851, however, this desire may have grown desperate since Catharine no longer had a family home to return to. Her stepmother and her father's second wife, Harriet, had died in 1835, and in 1836, Lyman Beecher married Lydia Beals Jackson. Catharine did not develop a close relationship with this new stepmother. To complicate things further, by the 1850s, Lyman Beecher was suffering from senility. In 1851, Lyman and Lydia left Cincinnati and retired in Boston. When she learned of her father's illness, Catharine offered to move in with Lyman and Lydia in order to care for her father. "I wish it could be so arranged that I could keep house, and you and he board with me. I could do twice as much *head* work if I could have the gentle exercise and the *amusement* of housekeeping," she wrote Lydia.[7] Catharine was hoping, she confided to her stepmother, to live with them so that she would not have to rent a room in Boston. But Lydia Beecher refused to allow Catharine to care for Lyman in any capacity. Catharine, who had spent much of her adulthood periodically living with her father, was now forbidden from residing in his house. Milwaukee, Catharine concluded, would have to replace her lost home.

Things went well at first. The Milwaukee Female Institute was a success. By 1852 the college had 120 students, four instructors, as well as a normal department to train students to be teachers, and a department of domestic economy—the precursor for home economics—that followed Beecher's educational plan. The school's curriculum offered the type of general education and specialty training she believed all young women needed and a permanent school building, which Beecher had designed, was under construction.

Everything was not as perfect as it seemed, however. The local trustees were initially unable to keep their promise to raise the money to pay for the construction of the permanent school building. Although this point had been key in her negotiations with the city of Milwaukee, Beecher did not see this as a crushing set back. She was, after all, a master fundraiser. In 1852 she founded the American Woman's Education Association as her new fundraising organization. Located in New York City, this group was made up of men and women who embraced Beecher's ideas. The women were housekeepers, mothers, and teachers, and the men were prominent businessmen. They represented a variety of Christian denominations, making the committee diverse for its time. The mission of the American Woman's Education Association included securing an endowment for the Milwaukee Female Institute.

Beecher's Achilles heel was, as always, that there was not enough money. While the trustees of the Milwaukee Female Institute did eventually pay off the construction loan and the American Woman's Educational Association successfully raised enough to pay for the salaries of the Milwaukee teachers and Beecher's traveling expenses for four years, neither group raised enough money to provide the necessary endowment. As if she had expected this, Beecher soon published two books on health, hoping that the royalties would financially sustain her mission as *Treatise* had and as she had intended *True Remedy for the Wrongs of Women* to do.

The first of these books on health, *Letters to the People on Health and Happiness*, reflected Beecher's interest in alternative medical treatments. Her initial interest in water cure had sparked an interest in other alternative medical treatments, especially those that focused on exercise to strengthen the body. Thus, by the mid-1850s, Beecher had begun practicing another alternative medical treatment: the movement cure. She was introduced to this treatment by her friend Elizabeth Blackwell, the first female physician in the United States. The movement cure was a practice geared to reverse the skeletal damage in women caused by wearing corsets.

Middle-class women of Beecher's generation were expected to wear corsets to shape their torso by cinching the waist. This undergarment was typically made from cotton and extended from the chest to the top of the hips. It was stiffened with boning inserted into the cloth. The corset was then held together by laces in the back that, when tightened, made the corset firmer. The overall effect was to make the waist appear smaller and the hips and bust larger, thereby creating the hourglass silhouette. While many physicians warned women that tightly laced corsets were bad for the health, this fashion denoted propriety, and was an important indication of social class, since it indicated the middle-class and elite women did not have to support themselves with physical labor, as their working-class counterparts did. Women began wearing corsets as children and continued through adulthood, even when pregnant.

The movement cure condemned corsets, arguing that wearing corsets caused the ribs to shift. Skeletal deformity due to corsets was a genuine concern for movement practitioners, who developed protocols for curing the physical damage they believed resulted from corset wearing. The cure centered around exercise and building muscle. Based on nineteenth-century understandings of anatomy, treatments included slapping, massaging, and shaking the torso to expand the chest and increase oxygen intake. Proponents claimed that a patient's chest could expand as much as four inches within months of beginning treatments.

Beecher, also a critic of corsets, participated in an eight-week residency at a movement cure facility in New York City. At the end of her stay, she claimed that she had to enlarge all her clothing two inches around the chest and three inches around the waist. She felt energetic for the first time in years. Unfortunately, shortly after leaving, Beecher was injured when her clothing became snagged on a moving railroad car. She was dragged and nearly pulled under the wheels of the train. The accident aggravated an injury to one of her limbs and, combined with the fright—and perhaps the stress of fundraising for the Milwaukee Female Institute—she had another nervous breakdown. Catharine Beecher was incapacitated for the next year.

Beecher did not record how she spent her time during the year she was recovering from her accident. She must have used it to write, because only one year later, in 1855, *Letters to the People on Health and Happiness* was published. Perhaps her injury had made women's health that much more important to Beecher, because the publication of *Letters to the People on Health and Happiness* signaled the beginning of her physical education campaign. She had written about exercise in her previous publications, but had linked good health to women's ability to fulfill domestic roles. By the time that *Letters to the People* was published, Beecher's arguments on the importance of health had evolved. It was women's profession to be caretakers of the home, she wrote, but also to protect the health of the family and thereby the nation.

Beecher opened *Letters to the People on Health and Happiness* by addressing her readers as "my friends." This literary technique was common among social reformers and was designed to build trust between the writer and audience. In this case, Beecher used the familiarity that many readers already had with her literary persona to explain that she was urging Americans to examine the health of women and children; both, she said, were becoming sicker. It was in *Letters* that Beecher's writings moved away from the Evangelical emphasis of her previous writings. Beecher had spent most of her adult life creating a culture for women that empowered them beyond what was allowed in religious dogma. Yet, while her writings had argued that women—not ministers—were the moral guardians of the nation, Beecher was still greatly influenced by Christianity. Now, in *Letters*, she established functional rather than religious guidelines for maintaining health.

The heart of *Letters to the People on Health and Happiness*, however, was to address the types of ailments afflicting Americans and offer solutions. In one particularly poignant chapter, Beecher used her own poor health to demonstrate how wellness could be achieved. As an infant, she explained, her development was delayed. She did not walk until she was two years old, and her earliest memories were of poor eyesight. As she grew, however, her health improved. She attributed this change to spending her childhood playing outdoors and eating a simple diet of bread, vegetables, fruits, milk, and meat. When she reached adulthood and began her career, the long sedentary hours working as a teacher affected her health. Her eyesight was once again weak, and she was often ill. She began to suffer from a nervous condition that caused temporary paralysis. At her sickest, Beecher recalled, she was unable to read, write, or speak. The moral, she told her readers, was that fresh air and exercise had once again restored her health.

Catharine Beecher's description of her health problems ultimately served as a cautionary tale about sedentary lifestyles and gluttonous eating habits. Here we can see the influence of water cure and the broader health reform movement on her. The goal of the health reform movement was to eradicate sin by creating healthy bodies, for it was believed that a diseased body reflected a diseased soul. It was from this movement that ideas of drinking water and exercising daily became mainstreamed. Reformers like Reverend Sylvester Graham advocated vegetarianism and diets of whole grains, specifically a dense, bran bread popularly referred to as "Graham bread" and "Graham crackers" –the forerunner to the modern, sweetened, whole-wheat cracker by the same name. Along with his colleague, Dr. William Alcott, Graham published multiple journal articles focused on the link between healthy eating and virtue. Later, Graham and Alcott's work would influence Dr. James C. Jackson to invent granola and Dr. John Harvey Kellogg to invent corn flakes. But food was only one part of health reform. Proponents also encouraged people to understand the fundamentals of health care. *Letters to the People on Health and Happiness* was in line with this agenda.

In publishing *Letters to the People on Health and Happiness* Beecher also accomplished something that the health reform community was unable to accomplish, appealing to a broad audience. Where *Treatise on Domestic Economy* had served as an instruction manual for housewives, *Letters to the People on Health and Happiness* was a lesson on restoring the physical health of the nation. And here Beecher added to the argument from *Treatise*, by claiming that a healthy body increased one's ability to maintain integrity. She also tasked women with raising healthy children, for vigorous children were the promise of a prosperous future of the United States.

How, though, were women to ensure the health of their families when they too were increasingly ill? To emphasize the extent to which women were sick, Beecher compiled statistics from her travels. A survey of 200 towns revealed that most women questioned suffered from headaches or were simply categorized as "feeble" and "delicate." Some women claimed they did not know one other woman who was healthy. In part, Beecher's statistics reflected the limitations of nineteenth-century medicine. Conditions that physicians now understand to be typical among women such as congestive heart failure and complications from multiple pregnancies were not always diagnosable and had limited treatments. Beecher also reiterated her suspicion of mainstream medicine, arguing that doctors' cures were often more detrimental than the ailment. After hearing Beecher speak one woman admitted:

> I see now why all I have suffered in mind and body from my physician is worse than useless. I see now that I have never had the disease for which I was treated. Is it not shocking that I should have suffered what was so needless, when my physician did our ought to have known better?[8]

Whether Beecher's advice truly revealed this woman's misdiagnosis is unclear, but her argument in favor of domestic medicine was part of a larger movement to help the public understand disease and to hold physicians accountable for their diagnoses.

The social impact of *Letters to the People on Health and Happiness* notwithstanding, it is also important to remember that this book was written as a fundraising tool for the Milwaukee Female Institute. In the final chapter, Beecher appealed to her readers to donate money to the Association of American Women. She reminded women that while ministers and doctors were influential in the community, women were the only ones who could keep a family healthy. Thus, the publication of *Letters* accomplished two goals for Beecher: it provided an additional justification for the importance of women's domestic role, and reminded readers of her ongoing fundraising efforts for women's education.

The year after *Letters to the People on Health and Happiness* was released Beecher published *Physiology and Calisthenics for Schools and Families*. This book was both another attempt at fundraising and the second volume in Beecher's physical culture campaign. The text was based on the calisthenics classes she taught at the Hartford Female School and the Milwaukee Female College. Beecher believed calisthenics could be incorporated into classrooms throughout the United States. She envisioned her book becoming a standard in classrooms across America

Physiology and Calisthenics for Schools and Families was divided into two sections, each with different exercises. These activities, Beecher explained in the introduction, were suitable for children as well as adults. The first section contained examples of fifty exercises that could be done behind a desk. This was followed by twelve exercises designed to be done in a large space such as an auditorium. Modern calisthenics uses one's body weight to exercise muscle groups. In Beecher's time, calisthenics was more like gentle aerobics. The exercises included in her book made an obvious nod to the types of exercises taught at water cure and movement cure institutions. She included instructions for arm and leg extensions, side bends, knee bends, and leg lifts. The more vigorous exercises included skipping, marching, balancing, and using light weights. Beecher wanted her regimen to be suitable for all fitness levels. However, she was careful to ensure that the exercise routines she promoted, which did little to build muscle, maintained the expectations of Victorian notions of femininity.

Throughout 1856 Beecher toured the country promoting *Physiology and Calisthenics for Schools and Families*. She arranged for portions of the book to be published in local newspapers prior to her arrival in each city. Once again, Beecher's celebrity preceded her, and the book tour was a success. By her own account, *Physiology and Calisthenics* was widely adopted by schools, and work would serve as one of the foundations of physical education courses. In 1856, *Peterson's Magazine* claimed that "no family should be without this valuable little book," while the *Connecticut Common School Journal* promised that the book would be "worth to any teacher far more than the entire cost of the book."[9] Five years later, Beecher was invited to give a speech at the Boston gymnasium owned by reformer Dr. Diocletion Lewis. Lewis was thrilled to host the great Catharine Beecher because, as he wrote, "Few have accomplished so much in the educational field."[10] She was also now known for her views on physical education.

The irony in Beecher publishing books on health and physical education was that she herself was so often ill. As she explained in *Letters*, however, her ability to understand what behaviors affected her health and correct them gave her arguments credence. This is also why her frequent visits to water cure institutions may have served the dual purpose of allowing her to convalesce while also establishing her as an authority on women's health. As she told her readers, "… in my extensive journeys and visits, I have come into the sphere of almost every kind of medical treatment, either by my own experiences or by that of my intimate friends."[11] But physical education was also not a new idea for Beecher. As a student at the Litchfield Academy, she had been encouraged to take daily walks, and when she opened the Hartford Female Seminary, exercise was included in the curriculum. Therefore, physical education became part of her broad plan to reform school curricula. She just hoped that she could financially benefit from her plan as well.

Beecher must have been pleased that her books were so well received. She had been so confident that these publications would provide the finances that she needed for the Milwaukee Female Institute endowment that she had preemptively asked the Milwaukee trustees to select a site for a cottage to house the Department of Domestic Economy. Since they had paid off the construction loan for the school building it must have seemed logical to Beecher that a new building project was feasible. The cottage that she requested would not only house the Department of Domestic Economy; it would also serve as a home for her. She was moving forward with her plan to retire in Milwaukee, and assumed that the trustees would gladly pay for the construction of the cottage if she contributed $3,000. This assumption proved wrong. The trustees rejected the request to pay for the house and advised Beecher that she would be better off paying the costs entirely by herself. She did not have the money, for her two books did not bring in the profits *Treatise* had. She was so deeply disappointed that she broke ties with the Milwaukee Female Institute and resigned from the American Woman's Educational Association.

Five years later, the trustees did construct a building for the Department of Domestic Economy and asked Beecher to head it. The home they offered her, however, was a dormitory rather than a private house. She refused it. Beecher's split with the Milwaukee Female Institute signaled the end of her career as an educator. Her failure to establish the stability for herself that she promised the Milwaukee teachers is indicative of the challenges female professionals of the era faced. Beecher had drawn a salary from the schools she ran, but without these educational positions she had no income. *Treatise* had temporarily brought in funds, but she had quickly spent them on her own ventures. None of her other books had sold as well. Now, Catharine Beecher, whose name was known in most middle-class households, was unable to live independently. She did not have the personal funds nor was she able to secure a job that would pay for housing. When she traveled, she stayed with friends or relatives. The rest of the time, without her father's home to return to, Beecher had to rely on her siblings for a home and financial support.

Beecher assumed that she was always welcome in her siblings' homes, but this did not prove to be the case. Although her protégées described Catharine as generous, family members saw her controlling, demanding, and too often thoughtless. In one instance, Beecher was asked to leave her niece's home after she fired the maids for refusing to cook recipes from her own cookbook. Catharine's sister, Isabella Beecher Hooker, found her both ill-mannered and self-centered. "Some weeks ago," Hooker wrote to Beecher,

> you sent me a line saying you would be here on such a day to attend a committee meeting—and you did not enquire whether my house was

full and your coming would be an inconvenience in any way, nor did you write in season for me to send any reply whatever.[12]

Isabella also chided here sister for giving all her money to charities instead of investing it in a home of her own. Worst of all, Hooker found Catharine was often a troublemaker, even if unintentionally. "You have repeatedly and over and over again," Isabella wrote, "discovered to cousins for instance differences and unfriendlinesses between them that they never thought of and which never existed save your imagination."[13] Beecher's only defense was to remind her sister that "A truly *Christian home* is not complete without aged or infirm members."[14] This did not change Isabella's view that Catharine suffered from a prickly personality.

Beecher's best relationship was with sister Harriet Beecher Stowe. The two had education and writing in common. Stowe had been a student as well as a teacher at the Harford Female Seminary and took over the school when Beecher left for Cincinnati in 1832. Throughout the 1830s, they wrote books together. In 1851, Stowe asked Beecher to spend a year with her family in Maine. Stowe needed someone to take over running her household and caring for her children while she labored over the writing of *Uncle Tom's Cabin*. Where once Harriet had confessed to her father and brother that she found Catharine "strange, nervous, visionary, and to a certain extent unstable," her appreciation of her sister had grown after reading *True Remedy for the Wrongs of Women*.[15] "I see now," Stowe wrote "that she has been busy for eight years about one thing."[16] Stowe encouraged her father and brother to read *True Remedy*, so they too could understand Beecher's educational mission. The education system that Beecher had designed was more advanced than any of them had realized, Stowe told them, explaining that:

> A system so extensive carried on by means of correspondence all over the country—dependent on an immense number of influences and agents from Maine to Georgia and from Massachusetts to Iowa *of course* would include *failures in particular parts*—and when one of these have occurred, many not seeing that they were only small parts of the great *whole* which was all the while moving on, have supposed that she was constantly attempting and constantly failing....[17]

Beecher was anything but a failure, Stowe insisted, and she deserved the respect of her family. This reassessment of Beecher's work likely influenced Stowe to open her home to her sister.

Beecher accepted her sister's invitation. Her year in Maine was primarily dedicated to improving the Stowe home. Together, she and Harriet ran a boarding school for the children of relatives. She used her own money to pay for repairs and furnishings while each day Stowe worked on her novel. Although the two sisters squabbled over the cost of the boarding school, they bonded over their mutual opposition to the dominance of men within Evangelical Protestantism.

The sisters were protective of one another, and openly critical of male authority they deemed unworthy. When *Uncle Tom's Cabin* sold 300,000 copies in the first year, Beecher pushed Stowe's publisher, John P. Jewett, to renegotiate the terms of her contract, which gave the publisher 90 percent of the royalties from the book. Beecher's three-year campaign to renegotiate Stowe's contract embarrassed much of the Beecher family. "Cate is making herself half sick about it," Isabella Beecher Hooker wrote to her husband,

> calls Jewett a scoundrel and with her usual pertinacity says she will make the matter public unless they adopt her view of the case. What a pity that she will meddle so—she is so anxious that Hatty [should] have the means of educating her three million children she won[']t rest till she has made trouble somewhere.[18]

Because of Beecher's influence, however, Stowe became a wealthy woman from the royalties of *Uncle Tom's Cabin*. Stowe understood that in taking on Jewett Beecher was challenging male authority. She had done as much, herself, when she publicly targeted the Reverend Joel Parker for justifying slavery in his rhetoric, going so far as to quote him in *Uncle Tom's Cabin*. When Parker threatened to sue her, Stowe refused to back down. Later, Calvin Stowe and Henry Ward Beecher negotiated a settlement with Parker, and Stowe removed the quotes from her novel, but her point was clear: the clergy did not have the best interest of women or African Americans at heart and should be held accountable. These intense reactions on the parts of Beecher and Stowe reflected their continued frustration with women's limited roles in America.

Their resentment was also rooted in being Beecher women for although they were proud of their family, they also disliked being denied careers as ministers because of their gender. When Beecher published *Duty of American Women* in 1845, it was Stowe who wrote to congratulate her. And when Stowe first considered writing a novel about slavery, it was Beecher in whom she confided. Their loyalty to one another throughout the 1850s exemplified the importance of women supporting one another's careers. While Beecher did not influence the writing of *Uncle Tom's Cabin*, her presence relieved Stowe of her domestic duties. Furthermore, *Uncle Tom's Cabin* was Stowe's attempt at appealing to slaveholders' empathies, demonstrating Beecher's point to Angelina Grimke in her *Essay on Slavery and Abolitionism* that women should use their benevolence to influence the opinions of those with whom they disagreed. Neither woman could fully anticipate, however, that *Uncle Tom's Cabin* would fuel the fire of regional dissent that led to civil war.

The issue of slavery gripped national politics throughout the 1850s. While Beecher was living with the Stowes in Maine, settlers in the West were adapting to the Compromise of 1850. This compromise was in response to questions about the role slavery would play in the western territories the United States had gained in 1848 at the conclusion of the Mexican War. Previously, the 1820 Missouri Compromise had settled this issue by allowing Missouri into the Union as a slave state and Maine as a free state. According to the Missouri Compromise, the status of new states entering the Union would be determined by whether they were above (free) or below (slave) the 36/30 longitude and latitude lines. While this agreement worked for decades, California's application for statehood in 1849 upset the delicate balance. California had become a territory of the United States in 1848 as part of the land gained from the Mexican War. One year later, gold was discovered in California, and American migrants and global immigrants flooded the territory in hopes of becoming rich. The growing population created a need for civil government and statehood. Geographically, however, California was both north and south of the 36/30 line. As a result, it was clear that a new political compromise had to be reached.

The resulting Compromise of 1850 was written by senators Henry Clay and Stephen Douglas in an attempt to avoid conflict between the North and South. There were five bills that made up the resulting compromise—slavery would be allowed in Washington DC, but slaves could not be traded there, California would enter the Union as a free state, the territories of Utah and New Mexico would determine whether slavery was allowed via popular sovereignty, geographic lines between Texas and Mexico were drawn, and the Fugitive Slave Act was strengthened. While the Compromise of 1850 settled the issue of slavery in California, the changes to the Fugitive Slave Act infuriated northern abolitionists. The Fugitive Slave Act was first passed in 1793, but specified only that anyone aiding runaway slaves would be penalized. The amended Fugitive Slave Act of 1850 now required that all citizens assist in the capture of escaped slaves. Many northern states refused to enforce the Fugitive Slave Act, further exacerbating the tensions with southern slaveholders who feared that abolitionists would successfully emancipate the enslaved. For Catharine Beecher, the Fugitive Slave Act also revealed the clergy's weakness in confronting the issue of slavery. "I have been mortified and astonished to see men of piety and men I thought *clear-headed* as befogged as I found them all over the country," she wrote.[19] But the Fugitive Slave Act was not the only issue that exacerbated regional fears over slavery. The popularity of Harriet Beecher Stowe's 1852 novel *Uncle Tom's Cabin* further played into southern slave holders' fears that northern abolitionists would successfully abolish slavery.

Harriet Beecher Stowe had published *Uncle Tom's Cabin* in 1852 as a condemnation of northern apathy and southern slaveholding based on her observations of the race riots and presence of escaped slaves in Cincinnati. The story of the kindly slave Uncle Tom, the innocent white girl Eva, runaway Eliza, the ignorant slave girl Topsy, and the brutal overseer Simon Legree pulled on the emotions of northern readers. The southern response was different. Southern diarist and slave owner Mary Boykin Chestnut noted that "Topsys I have known, but none that were beaten or ill-used. Evas are mostly in the heaven of Mrs. Stowe's imagination."[20] But even with southern criticisms, *Uncle Tom's Cabin* sold more copies than every book except the Bible. While by today's standards Stowe's portrayal of Black Americans is stereotypical, at the time, audiences were moved by the story. *Uncle Tom's Cabin* was so influential that upon meeting Stowe in 1862, during the Civil War, President Abraham Lincoln commented "So you're the little woman who wrote the book that started the great war!"[21] While there is no evidence that the Civil War began because of *Uncle Tom's Cabin*, it certainly did nothing to cool regional agitation.

In 1854, Two years after *Uncle Tom's Cabin* was published, national politics metaphorically exploded over the issue of slavery. Rather than pacify sectional tensions, the Compromise of 1850 had only worsened hostilities. This was also the year that the Republican Party was organized. Their platform was to limit the expansion of slavery. When Democratic politician Stephen Douglas proposed a bill to open new territorial lands so that a transcontinental railroad could be developed, the question of whether these areas would be slave or free arose once again. The subsequent Kansas-Nebraska bill created the territories of Kansas and Nebraska, but rather than adhere to the 36/30 slavery line, the bill specified that local elections would determine whether these regions were slave or free. This doctrine, known as popular sovereignty, nullified the Missouri Compromise. While popular sovereignty theoretically placed the power with the people, there were no safeguards to prevent residents from other regions from voting in these local elections. Slaveholders from Missouri repeatedly crossed territorial borders to fraudulently vote. The next few years in Kansas and Nebraska were characterized by open violence between pro- and anti-slavery settlers. Foreshadowing the Civil War, between 1854 and 1861, these confrontations were known as Bleeding Kansas.

The politics of Bleeding Kansas reverberated throughout the country. In 1855, Henry Ward Beecher, now the minister of Brooklyn's Plymouth Church, participated in a Hartford, Connecticut fundraiser for guns that would be sent to the frontier. Should twenty-five rifles be pledged, Beecher told the audience, Plymouth Church would pledge twenty-five more. Twenty-seven rifles were pledged in all. Several weeks later, a group of men calling themselves the "Beecher Bible and Rifle Company" traveled West with brand new Sharps rifles and Bibles, courtesy of Plymouth Church. The press, dubbed the rifles "Beecher's Bibles" and chastised Beecher for advocating violence. Unswayed, Henry Ward Beecher explained, "There are times when self-defense is a religious duty."[22] He was not alone in this belief. Violence between pro-slavery advocates and abolitionists would only escalate and Kansas would be at the center of the fighting.

Among the most well-known incidents of violence in Kansas occurred on May 21, 1856, when a group of pro-slavery raiders attacked the free town of

Lawrence. As the men demolished the town, they shouted, "The superiority of the White race!" and "Bibles not rifles!"[23] The town of Lawrence was sacked—buildings were burned, and the presses destroyed. The next day, Charles Sumner, a Republican senator from Massachusetts, denounced the Kansas-Nebraska Act in his "Crime Against Kansas Speech." Sumner specifically denounced the authors of the Act, inadvertently offending his fellow Senator, Preston Brooks of South Carolina, whose uncle was named. Two days later, Preston Brooks entered the Senate and beat Charles Sumner nearly to death with a cane. The same week, as Brooks' attack on Sumner the most famous altercation linked to Bleeding Kansas occurred in Kansas: The Pottawatomie Massacre. In reaction to the sacking of Lawrence, Kansas by pro-slavery supporters, abolitionist John Brown and a group of abolitionist settlers murdered five pro-slavery men.

The violence in Kansas made it clear that the enslaved would not easily gain their freedom in frontier states and territories. This was further clarified in 1857 when the Supreme Court ruled in the case of Dred Scott v. Sandford that the US Constitution did not extend citizenship to African Americans. The year after the Dred Scott decision, politicians Stephen Douglas and Abraham Lincoln participated in a series of seven debates on the issue of slavery. The country was becoming more polarized over whether the future of the nation included slavery and Henry Ward Beecher and Harriet Beecher Stowe were important figures in the abolitionist assault.

Catharine Beecher, however, was more worried about the morality of the nation than national politics. "Meanwhile," she wrote, "as men are losing the restraints of self-government, family discipline, and law, the causes of dangerous excitement are multiplying." Beecher envisioned this threat as,

> The clashing interests of foreigners and native-born citizens, the deep-rooted prejudices of Catholics and Protestants, the threatening aspects of slavery, the demoralizing influences of party politics and the political press, the all-pervading malaria of corrupt literature, the low tone of piety in the Christian church, the consequent increase of sectarian bitterness, and finally, the wide prevalence of rationalism, infidelity, and skepticism.

To Beecher, "all these present portentous omens of danger."[24] She believed the antidote for this poison in society was education. She pleaded with the press to pay as much attention to popular education as it did other social reforms because it was in the home and the schoolroom that the future of the nation resided. The heroes of her narrative were as always, women,

> For it is WOMAN who is to come in at this emergency, and meet the demand—woman, whom experience and testimony have shown to be the best, as well as the cheapest guardian and teacher of childhood, in school as well as the nursery…this is the way in which *a profession* is to be created

for women—a profession as lucrative for her as the legal, medical, and theological professions are for men.[25]

Even with the country on the brink of war, Beecher stayed true to her objective: promoting the causes of women in education was central to Beecher's identity, whether she was actively teaching or not. In focusing exclusively on the importance of domestic duties, she had forged an identity for middle-class women. From the 1850s onward, however, national discussions would become largely focused on issues of race and gender equality. Catharine Beecher would be forced to carve out her place in a nation no longer interested in her brand of conservative feminism.

Notes

1 Minerva Brace Norton, *A True Teacher: Mary Mortimer, a Memoir* (New York: Fleming H. Revell Company, 1894), 115.
2 Norton, 118.
3 Norton, 120.
4 Catharine Beecher, *The True Remedy for the Wrongs of Women with a History of An Enterprise Having that for its Object* (Boston: Philips, Sampson & Co., 1851), 152.
5 C. Beecher, *True Remedy for the Wrongs of Women*, 152.
6 C. Beecher, *True Remedy for the Wrongs of Women*, 154.
7 Kathryn Kish Sklar, *Catharine Beecher: A Study in American Domesticity* (New York: W.W. Norton & Company, 1976), 220.
8 "Communication from Mrs. Dr. R.B. Gleason," in *Letters to People on Health and Happiness*, Note I (New York: Harper & Brothers Publishers, 1855), 9.
9 "Physiology and Calisthenics," *Peterson's Magazine* (May 2, 1856), 401.
10 Dio Lewis, "Miss Beecher and her Western College," *Lewis' New Gymnastics for Ladies, Gentleman and Children and the Boston Journal of Physical Culture* (August 1861), 155.
11 Catharine Beecher, *Letters to the People on Health and Happiness* (New York: Harper & Brothers Publishers, 1855), 120.
12 Isabella Beecher Hooker to Catharine Beecher, May 9, 1869, in Jeanne Boydstron, et.al. eds., *The Limits of Sisterhood: The Beecher Sisters on Women's Rights and Woman's Sphere* (Chapel Hill: The University of North Carolina Press, 1988), 351.
13 Isabella Beecher Hooker to Catharine Beecher, May 9, 1869, in The *Limits of Sisterhood*, 351.
14 Catharine Beecher to Isabella Beecher Hooker, May 9, 1869, in *The Limits of Sisterhood*, 352.
15 Harriet Beecher Stowe to Lyman and Henry Ward Beecher, September 19. 1851 in *The Limits of Sisterhood*, 345.
16 Ibid.
17 Ibid.
18 Isabella Beecher Hooker to John Hooker, June 26, 27, 1852 in *The Limits of Sisterhood*, 348–349.
19 Sklar, 235.
20 Mary Chestnut, *Mary Chestnut's Civil War*, ed. C. Vann Woodward (New Haven: Yale University Press, 1981), 307–308.
21 Joan D. Hedrick, *Harriet Beecher Stowe: A Life* (New York: Oxford University Press, 1994), Location 9. Kindle.

22 Debby Applegate, *The Most Famous Man in America: The Biography of Henry Ward Beecher* (New York: Doubleday Press, 2006), 281–282.
23 Applegate, 282.
24 C. Beecher, *The True Remedy for the Wrongs of Women*, 236.
25 C. Beecher, *True Remedy for the Wrongs of Women*, 241.

8
THE FINAL PHASE

After her 1856 break with the Milwaukee Female Institute, Catharine Beecher once again found her career at a standstill. And so, she dealt with this uncertainly as she had many times before; she made sense of her world by writing about it. Her books from the late 1850s through the 1870s repeated many points made in her earlier publications, but they also forged a new identity for Beecher, one based less on Christianity and more on secularism. And so, as she entered the last phase of her life, she reframed her arguments for a new audience. She hoped that American culture was changing, and she knew she must modernize her course, or be left behind.

By the time that she left Milwaukee in 1856 Beecher had begun writing a new book on religion. Her views had evolved; they were no longer based on theology but on humanitarianism. She had always had a conflicted relationship with religion. She remembered that as a child "I was taught to look at God as a great 'moral governor,' whose chief interest was to 'sustain his law.'"[1] As an adult, she both lamented the fact that she could not become a minister like her father and brothers, and resented the authority given to the clergy. Her refusal to conform to orthodox religious thought had made her relationship with her father difficult when she was young. Now, at almost sixty years old, Catharine Beecher was willing to confront religion anew. Perhaps this had something to do with her father's senility, for it meant she would not have to debate Lyman. But Beecher was a very different person than she had been as a young woman, and she had been developing her theories for more than a quarter century.

In 1857 the first of two volumes outlining Beecher's views on religion, *Common Sense Applied to Religion, or the Bible and the People*, was published. Two years later, the second volume, *An Appeal to the People on Behalf of Their Rights as Authorized Interpreters of the Bible* appeared. Within these volumes Beecher

DOI: 10.4324/b23305-9

questioned organized religion by analyzing the concepts of redemption and damnation as they applied to social situations, not theology. "Again, our minds come into existence in a *social system* so constituted that the rewards and penalties of law extend, not merely to the good and evil doer, but to those connected with him," Beecher wrote, "Thus each mind is made dependent for happiness on the well-doing of those around almost as much as on its own obedience to law."[2] Everyone had the ability to distinguish right from wrong by using reason, Beecher told her readers, and American society would continue to progress as long as people prioritized the needs of the many over the few.

For Beecher, these publications were part of her long journey toward making peace with religion. Perhaps writing these books was the final push she needed to leave Calvinism behind, for in 1862 Catharine Beecher and three of Harriet Beecher Stowe's daughters were confirmed in the far more liberal Episcopal Church. Stowe would later join the faith as well. Beecher continued to view the world in terms of good and evil and to argue that self-sacrifice was the guiding force toward good. As the Civil War neared, she saw more and more evidence that only self-sacrifice would save the nation.

Although Beecher remained more aloof from national politics than her famous siblings Harriet Beecher Stowe and Henry Ward Beecher, she was well aware that regional tensions were escalating throughout the 1850s. When Republican Abraham Lincoln was elected president in the fall of 1860, South Carolina responded by seceding from the United States. Between December 1860 and April 1861, ten other southern states joined the new nation, the Confederate States of America. The secession of southern states was motivated by a certainty that the election of a Republican president threatened the institution of slavery. Yet Abraham Lincoln did not immediately take an antislavery stance. In his 1861 inaugural address he argued for the preservation of the Union, not the end of slavery. Later that spring, his desire to save the Union led Lincoln to send ships to supply Fort Sumter, off the South Carolina coast. In response, a southern militia fired on the fort. Lincoln then asked for 75,000 militia volunteers to enlist for three months. The Civil War had begun.

No family was excluded from the hardships of the war, and the Beechers were no exception. Catharine Beecher's half-brother James and numerous nephews enlisted in the Union Army. When Henry Ward Beecher's underage son asked for permission to enlist, Beecher told him "If you don't, I'll disown you."[3] Henry dealt with the hardships of the war by throwing himself into the war effort. As a preacher, writer, and editor he had immense influence during the 1860s. Initially, he used that influence to support Abraham Lincoln's presidency. By 1862, however, he was disillusioned by Union defeats in battle and by Lincoln's reluctance to prioritize emancipation. He openly criticized the President in the journal he edited. "What has Mr. Lincoln's education done for him—more than ours for us—to fit him to judge of military affairs?" Henry Ward Beecher wrote,

We are sick and weary of this conduct. We have a sacred cause, a noble army, good officers, and a heroic common people. But we are like to be ruined by an administration that will not tell the truth...that is cutting and shuffling the cards for the next great political campaign.[4]

Thomas Beecher warned his brother that these tirades were counterproductive, since many men might be discouraged to enlist if they believed the war was about emancipation. Thomas had a point. Many northern men enlisted in the Union Army to preserve the Union, not to free the enslaved. It was only after these men saw the horrors of southern slavery for themselves that many of them shifted their view on the purpose of the war. Even Harriet Beecher Stowe, who was also a critic of Lincoln, questioned her brother's cynicism.

As the author of *Uncle Tom's Cabin*, Stowe was automatically viewed as an authority on the issue of emancipation. Her book was now published internationally, and her fame had grown. From the start of the war, Stowe had argued that emancipation must be its goal. Like Henry Ward Beecher, she wrote editorials openly criticizing Lincoln. When she heard that Lincoln had a plan to free the enslaved, she insisted that she must speak with him to verify his intentions. In 1862 Stowe, with three of her children and Isabella Beecher Hooker—also an outspoken proponent of emancipation—met with President Lincoln in Washington, DC. Although the details of the conversation have been lost to history, Stowe left the meeting convinced that Lincoln was a good man. Hooker too felt that Lincoln's "sincerity & pathos of character were both visible."[5] We do not know what influence Stowe may have had on Lincoln, but in the fall of 1862, Lincoln signed the Emancipation Proclamation.

The Emancipation Proclamation took effect on January 1, 1863, and freed enslaved people living within the Confederate States of America. Technically, Lincoln had no authority to free enslaved persons within the Confederacy and the Proclamation ignored the status of bondspeople in the five Union border states where slavery was legal– Delaware, Maryland, Kentucky, West Virginia, and Missouri. Yet the Emancipation Proclamation signaled a crucial shift in Lincoln's military and political strategy. The Civil War was no longer simply about maintaining the Union; it was about freeing the enslaved. Henry Ward Beecher was vindicated. And whether Harriet Beecher Stowe influenced the Emancipation Proclamation or not, her abolitionist friends credited her with the antislavery victory. At an 1863 abolitionist gathering to celebrate the Emancipation Proclamation the crowd chanted "Harriet Beecher Stowe!" until she rose to acknowledge them.[6]

But the Beecher family's patriotism could not prevent the desolation of the war from penetrating their lives. 1863 was a particularly trying year for the family. In January, Lyman Beecher died after a decade of senility. That July, Charles Beecher's son, Frederick, was severely wounded at the Battle of Gettysburg, as was Harriet and Calvin Stowe's son, also named Frederick. Frederick Stowe's wound was less severe than his cousin's. He had been shot in the ear. The wound never fully healed, however, and contributed to Stowe's alcoholism. Other tragedies plagued the Beecher's throughout the next decade. Although Frederick Beecher survived the Civil War, he was killed in 1868, fighting in the Indian Wars on the western frontier. His death occurred only a year after his twin sisters drowned. Frederick Stowe too met a tragic end. Though his family sent him to water-cure facilities to dry out and even institutionalized him, he was never able to control his drinking. Stowe finally disappeared in 1871. While his death was never confirmed, it is likely that he either succumbed to alcoholism or committed suicide.

These misfortunes must have affected Catharine Beecher as they did her siblings, but she gave no indication of her feelings in her writings. Instead, she focused on analyzing the Civil War as the ultimate example of the conflict between good and evil. The war also illustrated the importance of self-sacrifice. Beecher articulated this view in her 1864 publication *Religious Training of Children in the School, the Family, and the Church*. To her readers, she presented the country as a dangerous place, where slavery had made white men greedy and selfish. She condemned Christians for not taking a stand but praised the Union Army for demonstrating their morality as they figuratively combated southern vices on the battlefield. Beecher wrote,

> In this grand emergency, what deeds of self-sacrifice, what developments of heroic devotion have been evolved! Hundreds and thousands have given up ease, and home, and money-making, and been enrolled to offer life itself to save from these merely earthly dangers.

Women, she took care to point out, had a special role to play in the crisis. "In the family circle, too, the needle and all the outdoor implements of labor are enlisted in the same effort to raise the funds and supply the needs of this vast array who are to accomplish this great salvation."[7] There is no evidence, however, that the Civil War changed Beecher's views on abolition. Unlike her siblings, Henry Ward Beecher, Harriet Beecher Stowe, and Isabella Beecher Hooker, Catharine made no direct reference to emancipation in her writings. Instead, she summarized the Civil War's purpose in broader, grander terms. It was a means to "save, not our country alone, but the *whole world*, not from temporal, but from eternal dangers."[8] The four years of war seemed to be her "prophecy fulfilled."[9]

The Civil War officially ended on April 8, 1865, when the Confederate General Robert E. Lee surrendered to the Union General Ulysses S. Grant at Appomattox Court House in Virginia. The war had lasted four grueling years and had cost approximately 800,000 lives. The following week, the American flag was returned to Fort Sumter, and President Lincoln chose Henry Ward Beecher to give the ceremonial address. This was a high point in Henry's career, but his glory would be short-lived. The following day, Abraham Lincoln was assassinated by Confederate supporter John Wilkes Booth at Ford's Theater. In memorial, Harriet Beecher Stowe published a tribute to Lincoln describing him as "a new kind of ruler on the earth. There has been something even unearthly about his extreme unselfishness, his utter want of personal ambition, personal self-valuation, personal feeling."[10] Stowe's earlier criticisms of Lincoln had then vanished. In this, she was not alone. Lincoln's assassination made a martyr of the president. He would henceforth be remembered as "The Great Emancipator" rather than a man whose decision to free the slaves had developed gradually over time.

When the Civil War ended in 1865, slavery ended as well. Between 1865 and 1870 a series of three amendments to the Constitution—known as the Reconstruction Amendments—legally ended the institution of slavery. In 1865 the Thirteenth Amendment to the United States Constitution formally abolished slavery. Three years later the Fourteenth Amendment extended citizenship to former slaves, and in 1870, the Fifteenth Amendment gave Black men the right to vote. For more than a decade following the Civil War, however, the United States would be in a period of reconstruction.

During the Reconstruction Era the Federal Government worked to re-incorporate the former Confederate States back into the Union. Polarization between the Democratic President Andrew Johnson—who created policies to limit the rights of African Americans while empowering White southerners—and the Radical Republicans in Congress—who promoted Black Civil Rights—led to inconsistent legislation, often at the expense of the recently freed African Americans. Although there were moments of racial victory during Reconstruction, including a period where African American men held elected office at the local, state, and federal level, for many people race relations had not improved. When Reconstruction ended in 1877 the South passed legislation once again limiting the freedoms of African Americans. The resulting Black codes, popularly known as the Jim Crow Laws, legalized segregation and disenfranchised Black men. Vigilante groups such as the Ku Klux Klan enforced these laws with terrorism, making the fight for equal rights dangerous as well as controversial. It would be 100 years before the United States government enforced racial integration and protected African Americans' right to vote.

Like many American families, the Beecher siblings were also politically polarized during Reconstruction. Their political activism had not waned with the end of the Civil War, although the family hoped peace would soon follow. Despite his endorsement of violence, a decade earlier, Henry Ward Beecher promoted a policy of conciliation toward the South while Harriet Beecher Stowe, embittered by her son's Frederick's injury, condemned former Confederates. She was eventually swayed by Henry to promote peace. This decision had effects outside of the family. The fame of Henry Ward Beecher and Harriet Beecher Stowe meant that newspapers printed their views, and they frequently wrote for periodicals. Their opinions mattered to regular people and the Radical Republicans hoped that an endorsement for broad civil rights from Beecher and Stowe would further their cause. They were disappointed. While Henry and Harriet supported Black male suffrage, they did so on the condition that these men meet property and education requirements.

Meanwhile, as the country struggled to understand what it meant for African Americans to be free, Catharine Beecher continued her mission to train women as wives and mothers. Just as she had ignored the influence of abolition and immigration on national politics in previous decades, Beecher did so now as well. She also returned to Hartford. Catharine had been living with various Beecher relatives since her departure from Milwaukee in 1856, but now she moved in permanently with her sister Harriet Beecher Stowe. Her relationship with Stowe had become distant during the war years, due to the demands on Harriet's time as the author of *Uncle Tom's Cabin*. But in 1869, the sisters were reunited. By now, the Stowes had moved to Nook Farm in Hartford, Connecticut. It was here the sisters' intimacy was restored as they worked on a book project together. It would be published as *American Women's Home*, a sequel to *Treatise on Domestic Economy*.

In many ways, *American Women's Home* repeated the contents of *Treatise*. But in the years since that book's first publication American culture had changed. *Treatise* had been a response to expanding democracy and focused on a need to define women's place in this new social structure. The goal of *American Women's Home*, on the other hand, was to reestablish the importance of women's roles. Like Treatise, this work asserted that domesticity was a female profession. In the introduction, Beecher declared:

> It is the aim of this volume to elevate both the honor and the remuneration of all the employments that sustain the many difficult and sacred duties of the family state, and thus to render each department of woman's true profession as much desired and respected as are the most honored professions of men.

But the home was no longer exclusively the woman's domain, Beecher and Stowe argued. Men and women were both responsible for the care of the children. "...Implanted in the heart of every true man," they explained "is the desire for a home of his own, and the hopes of paternity."[11] The family was described aa a microcosm of society in which each person had a particular role to play; the stronger members of the family (parents) helping the weaker members (children). The older children would then, in turn, help care for the younger. Eventually, adult children would care for elderly parents. This was a radical change from the 1840s—when the home was exclusively the realm of the woman.

The publication of *American Women's Home* coincided with Beecher and Stowe's decision to re-open the Hartford Seminary in 1870. For Catharine Beecher, moving to Hartford had been a homecoming. She was reunited with her old social circle and spent her evenings playing charades or entertaining friends by parodying sermons. Guests might be invited to the Stowe home to enjoy "a door-step concert at Nook Farm with Miss Beecher at the guitar."[12] Perhaps it was initially nostalgia that led Beecher and Stowe to revive the Hartford Female Seminary. But support for women's education had grown significantly since the 1820s, and this made the revival of the Hartford School a timely endeavor.

When Beecher first opened the Hartford Female Seminary in 1823, she was pushing against gender boundaries by teaching subjects such as mathematics to females and measuring learning by comprehension rather than recitation. Now, academies were becoming like the seminary public high schools. In New York State, for example, at least sixty-four academies had been converted to high schools between 1853 and 1874. Those schools that maintained their status as tuition-charging academies now had to compete with free public high schools. Many survived by becoming state normal schools. The Hartford Female Seminary, however, remained private. It could not compete with newer schools, but Catharine and Harriet hoped that by once again linking their names to it, the Hartford Female Seminary could reclaim its former glory. Catharine Beecher invested $1,000 into the school, took on the role of principal, and moved into the house where the other teachers and students boarded. Harriet Beecher Stowe and Calvin Stowe helped with curriculum and lectured at the school

This seems to have been a happy time for Catharine Beecher. One student remembered that "She had a keen sense of humor and such a kind friendly manner that we all loved her."[13] Perhaps this was a chance for Beecher to achieve personal closure when it came to the Hartford School. It was certainly an opportunity for her to care for the boarders as she might if she was running her own household. She served them school lunches made of warm "Graham" Muffins based on an adaptation of health reformer Sylvester Graham's dietary suggestions. At dinner, Beecher sat at the head of the table and addressed the girls in French so that they could practice their language skills, although a former student remembered that Beecher was anything but fluent, herself. In the evenings she organized parlor dances. Yet this old-fashioned approach was not appreciated by all. Another student remembered that while the girls ultimately respected Beecher, they also made fun of her behind her back. Catharine Beecher's methods for educating and nurturing her students were antiquated, and she had become a beloved relic.

Inevitably the second iteration of the Hartford School was not as popular as the first. Beecher's methods were old fashioned and her lectures on student propriety were outdated. In the end, however, Beecher's main problem was not her pedagogy; it was in her inability to agree with the school trustees about money. True to her experience with every other school she had founded, Catharine insisted on an endowment, but the trustees refused to provide it. Beecher worked at the Hartford Female Seminary for only a year before turning its care over to a cousin. By the late nineteenth-century, the Seminary was more an artifact of an earlier era than a functioning school.

Despite her inability to fully revitalize the Hartford Female Seminary, Beecher was invigorated by the effort. Reopening the Hartford Female Seminary had offered her the chance to return to her first love: teaching. She may have also been responding to the gains in women's education following the Civil War, as an increasing number of co-educational and women's institutions were founded. After leaving the Hartford Female Seminary she spent the next two years fundraising for new women's universities.

While Beecher was busy raising money for women's colleges, her siblings were becoming embroiled in a rivalry between factions of the woman's suffrage movement. By 1870, the woman suffrage movement had splintered. The introduction of the word "male" into the Constitution through the Fourteenth Amendment and the exclusion of woman suffrage from the Fifteenth Amendment had left many woman rights activists feeling betrayed. Many of these women had been stanch abolitionists and felt that their Black male counterparts should have campaigned harder for women's suffrage to be included in the Reconstruction Amendments. Elizabeth Cady Stanton specifically lashed out against the Black community, arguing that White women were more deserving of suffrage than African Americans. She failed to acknowledge that while Black men legally had the right to vote, they were prevented from exercising that right by violence and intimidation. In response to criticism like Stanton's, abolitionist Frederick Douglass declared:

> When women, because they are women, are dragged from their homes and hung upon lampposts; when their children are torn from their arms and their brains dashed upon the pavement, when they are the objects of insult and outrage at every turn; when they are in danger of having their homes burnt down over their heads, when their children are not allowed to enter schools, then they will have [the same] urgency to obtain the ballot.[14]

Stanton, seemingly unmoved by Douglass, snapped back "Do you believe the African race is composed entirely of males?"[15] For Stanton and her suffrage partner, Susan B. Anthony, it was imperative that women's issues be given a national platform. Together they organized the all-female National Woman Suffrage Association (NWSA). The NWSA focused primarily on suffrage, but it also argued for women's right to education and divorce. Isabella Beecher Hooker was a dedicated follower of Elizabeth Cady Stanton and Susan B. Anthony and regularly published articles in the NWSA journal, *The Revolution*.

Not all suffragists agreed with Elizabeth Cady Stanton and Susan B. Anthony's radical stance, however. Their colleague Lucy Stone saw Black male suffrage as an important victory in the long fight for racial and gender equality; what benefited one group, Stone believed, would surely benefit the other. She broke with Stanton and Anthony and formed the American Woman Suffrage Association

(AWSA). The AWSA was more moderate than the NWSA. It focused exclusively on the vote and included male and female members. Henry Ward Beecher was the organization's first president.

Isabella Beecher Hooker and Henry Ward Beecher's opposing viewpoints on suffrage created tension within the family. That tension was heightened when Isabella Beecher Hooker organized the first suffrage convention in Hartford in 1869. Her goal was to reunite the NWSA and the AWSA. She convinced Harriet and Calvin Stowe to serve as vice presidents of the Connecticut Woman Suffrage Association, which would be launched during the Convention. Harriet Beecher Stowe remained unaffiliated with either the NWSA or the AWSA, although both organizations claiming her.

Hooker's attempts to reconcile the organizations failed. Afterward, Henry Ward Beecher was critical of Hooker's association with Stanton and Anthony and antagonized her by repeating inflammatory statements made by Lucy Stone. Despite this family tension, Isabella and her husband John Hooker remained dedicated to the woman's rights movement. Over the next few years, they were instrumental in petitioning the Connecticut legislature to pass property rights for women. While Henry and Isabella bickered over how suffrage should be achieved and Harriet remained neutral, Catharine Beecher continued to oppose votes for women. She joined the first anti-suffrage association, the Anti-Sixteenth Amendment Society.

The Anti-Sixteenth Amendment Society, named because women's suffrage was a proposed Sixteenth Amendment, had been formed by the writer Madeleine Vinton Dahlgren in 1869. This organization argued that the vote undermined marriage and motherhood. The society also claimed that women already had more than enough responsibilities with their domestic duties. Should women vote, it would cause marital discord, which may lead to divorce and irreparable harm to the children. This concern would later be voiced by anti-suffragists in the early twentieth century. This organization was short-lived, but members were able to accrue at least 5,000 signatures supporting a petition against suffrage. The petition was presented to Congress in 1871.

Catharine Beecher was among the more famous members of the Anti-Sixteenth Amendment Society. Her denunciation of woman suffrage was not surprising given her long held belief that men and women were fundamentally different. She agreed with suffragists that women's social importance was equal to men's, but she disagreed that equal legal and political rights were necessary. Beecher also worried that women would not be responsible voters. In an 1870 debate with suffragist Mary Livermore, she asked whether women would simply vote for the same candidate as the men in their lives. She conceded that woman might need to vote if a family emergency prevented a man from doing so, but she could think of no emergency great enough to necessitate that situation. Beecher reminded her audience that a woman's greatest strength lay in her unique feminine character. She insisted that woman's place was in the home; if she wanted more power she must look to education and not the ballot. In 1872 Beecher published her portion of the debate with Livermore as *Woman's Profession as Mother and Educator with Views in Opposition to Woman Suffrage*.

Beecher had always been uncompromising in her beliefs. Now in her 70s, it was clear she had no intention of updating her position on social reform or woman's rights. Her views, however, incited criticism from suffragists, specifically Victoria Woodhull.

Victoria Woodhull was one of the most famous women in America by 1870. She was known for her intelligence and beauty, but also for her radical social views. Woodhull had grown up in a starkly different world than the Evangelical Beecher home. Her father was a small-time conman who hired his children out as mystics. Together with her sister, Tennessee Claflin, young Victoria made money for the family by hosting séances, telling fortunes, and by faith healing. As an adult, she became notorious for her radical social ideas, especially her endorsement of free love. During the twentieth century free love would become associated with the counterculture of the 1960s and the sexual revolution, but during the nineteenth-century free love denoted romantic relationships unrestricted by the legal ties of marriage. It is likely that Woodhull's viewpoints on marriage were shaped by her own experience.

Woodhull met her first husband, Canning Woodhull, when she was fourteen, and he was twenty-eight. Canning was a doctor, and claimed to be from a prestigious New York political family. This probably impressed young Victoria. They were married within months. It is likely that Victoria Woodhull married to escape her abusive father, but her marriage was no respite. Her new husband was a physically abusive alcoholic and a womanizer. He had also lied about his pedigree and his profession. Canning Woodhull was not, in fact, a doctor, although he had been practicing medicine. He was also un-related to the New York political elite with whom he had claimed familial ties. Woodhull was penniless, and his drinking prevented him from working to support his family. Victoria Woodhull was often the one who worked outside of the home, even after the birth of their two children, one of whom was intellectually disabled. She finally procured a divorce from her husband in 1866, 11 years into her marriage. Divorces were not easy to obtain during the nineteenth-century, but by 1860, most states would accept habitual drunkenness and desertion as sufficient grounds. Canning Woodhull was guilty of both.

Although the law deemed Woodhull justified in her desire to end her marriage, she was not spared the social stigma attached to divorce. Ministers warned that to take more than one partner in a lifetime, without having been widowed, was immoral. Conservative theorists like Catharine Beecher understood marital separation to be sometimes necessary, but she opposed the dissolution of marriage. "A woman may separate from her husband for abuse or drunkenness & not violate [the law of marriage]," Beecher wrote, "but in such cases, neither party can marry again without practically saying I do not recognize Jesus Christ as the true teacher of morals & religion."¹⁶ Woodhull saw things differently and insisted that many—perhaps including her own—husbands raped their wives. She likened marriage to slavery. Woman's rights advocates including Elizabeth Cady Stanton and Harriet Beecher Stowe had used the same analogy between marriage and slavery when arguing for woman's rights. The difference, however, was that Stanton and Stowe applied the term slavery as a metaphor. Victoria Woodhull meant it literally. In her view, sexual relationships should be based solely on love. To Woodhull, the ability to change romantic partners at will was part of one's individual rights.

After her divorce, Victoria Woodhull and her sister, Tennessee Claflin, established themselves in New York City. There they worked as faith healers and mediums. After the Civil War, spiritualism—which taught that the living could contact the dead—became immensely popular with grieving families hoping to communicate with loved ones killed in the war. The Beecher siblings were among those caught up in the movement. Through their spiritualist work, Woodhull and Claflin met railroad baron Cornelius Vanderbilt. Vanderbilt distrusted mainstream medicine, preferring instead the care of healers, and regularly consulted spiritualists to communicate with his dead parents. When Vanderbilt met Woodhull and Claflin he was also a recent widower. While Tennessee Claflin tended to Vanderbilt's body, Victoria Woodhull passed along messages "from the spirit world" regarding stock market trends. In reality, Woodhull received business tips from New York City prostitutes, whose clients often bragged about their business dealings. Vanderbilt may or may not have been aware of Woodhull's sources, but he nevertheless became a patron for Woodhull and Claflin. By this time, he had begun having an affair with Tennessee Claflin. He paid the sisters generously for their services as mediums and gave them seed money to open a financial brokerage on Wall Street.

Victoria Woodhull and Tennessee Claflin were the first female stockbrokers in the United States. Nicknamed the "Bewitching Brokers" by the press, the sisters made their money by investing on behalf of women, whose business male brokers typically dismissed. A sign inside the door of their office read "Gentlemen Will State Their Business and Retire at Once."¹⁷ Vanderbilt also funded the women's newspaper dedicated to free love, the *Woodhull and Claflin Weekly*. Victoria Woodhull and Tennessee Claflin were unapologetically pushing against the social boundaries assigned their gender. If the Beecher family was an American institution, Woodhull and Claflin were the ultimate outsiders.

Victoria Woodhull refused to remain on the fringes of society, however. She was interested in politics and the financial stability she earned from Wall Street afforded her the opportunity to support a cause she held close to her heart: suffrage. In 1871—the same year that the Anti-Sixteenth Amendment Society sent their anti-suffrage petition to Congress—Woodhull became the first woman to address Congress. She appeared before a House Committee to argue that an amendment for woman suffrage should be passed. Woodhull did not bother to inform the organized suffrage movement of her plan. But Susan B. Anthony saw the potential value of recruiting Woodhull. "If it takes youth, beauty, and money to capture Congress," she declared. "Victoria is the woman we are after."[18] Isabella Beecher Hooker was also in the audience that day and she was moved by Woodhull's speech. For Hooker, Woodhull was "heaven sent for the rescue of women from her pit of subjugation."[19] Other suffragists were concerned that Woodhull's sordid reputation and association with free love would damage their cause. Harriet Beecher Stowe and Catharine Beecher were among those skeptical of any association with Woodhull. They made it their mission to convince Isabella that Woodhull was not a fit associate for a Beecher.

For her part, Victoria Woodhull was also critical of Catharine Beecher's anti-suffrage view. In the *Woodhull and Claflin Weekly*, she argued that it was unjust that women should pay taxes but be denied the vote. According to Woodhull it was "the Catherine (*sic*) Beechers who now clog the wheels of progress, and stand forth as enemies of their sex…these miserable women traitors to women ..these Miss Beecher women especially…" had stalled the woman's rights movement.[20]

Catharine Beecher's push for equal education for women during the 1820s had been a precursor to the woman's rights movement. Now, as Beecher neared the end of her life, Victoria Woodhull labeled her an obstruction to women's advancement. It was true that while Beecher had spent decades publishing books promoting her educational theories, other women's rights reformers had looked to politics to further their cause. This was exactly the type of activism Beecher had always denounced.

For women like Woodhull, the cult of domesticity had never been viable, and so she rejected the domestic sphere and Beecher's view of it. In turn, Beecher rejected Woodhull as the antithesis of true womanhood. Isabella Beecher Hooker insisted, however, that the women would change their minds if they knew each other personally. Perhaps they could even become friends. Catharine, Hooker wrote a friend, believed that Woodhull was a good person, albeit misguided in her belief in free love. Perhaps with Beecher's influence, Woodhull might tone down some of her beliefs. Likewise, Hooker hoped that Woodhull might change Beecher's views on the suffrage movement. In February 1871, Hooker played intermediary between Woodhull and Beecher, arranging for them to meet in New York City and share a carriage ride through Central Park. Hooker's matchmaking, however, would go terribly wrong.

From the start, Beecher was hostile toward Woodhull. She recounted that her first impression was that Woodhull was "either insane or a hapless victim of malignant spirits." According to Beecher, Woodhull

> calmly informed me that several distinguished editors, clergymen and lady authors of this city, some of them my personal friends, and all of them models of domestic purity and virtue, not only held her opinion on free love, but practiced accordingly, and that it was only a lack of moral courage which prevented their open avowal of such an opinion.[21]

Beecher rebuked Woodhull, lecturing her on the importance of women's subordination to men. According to Woodhull, it was then that she had a vision of "a band of devils with rat tails dancing around Miss Beecher's head."[22] Both women believed the other was possessed, and their conversation quickly became more contentious. Woodhull challenged Beecher's assertion that marriage was divine. She insisted that many people practiced free love in private, including Beecher's own brother, Henry Ward Beecher. Henry, Woodhull charged, was involved in an extramarital affair, an affair that proved her point that lifelong marriage was outdated and should be eliminated. "I do not condemn him," she told Catharine, "I applaud him. Would that he had the courage to join me in preaching what he practices." Catharine was appalled. "Evil!" she cried, but Woodhull insisted it was true. Beecher denied the accusation, then tried to explain that Henry was in an unhappy marriage. Victoria Woodhull refused to excuse him, instead arguing that the status of his marriage only proved her theories on free love. It was then that Beecher fully lost her temper. She began calling Woodhull names and as the two parted Catharine said "Remember, Victoria Woodhull, that I shall strike you dead!" Woodhull, unfazed, replied "Strike as much and as hard as you please, only don't do it in the dark, so that I cannot know who is my enemy." Likely flustered, Catharine repeated her threat, "I will strike you in every way; I can and will kill you, if possible."[23] Both women would later repeat this story for newspapers in an attempt to slander the other.

Isabella Beecher Hooker may have had an inclination that her sister, Catharine, would not get along with Victoria Woodhull. "Sister Catharine returned last night," Hooker wrote.

> She saw Victoria and, attacking her on the marriage question, got such a black eye as filled her with horror and amazement. I had to laugh inwardly at her relation of the interview and am now waiting for her to cool down![24]

What Hooker may not have understood, however, was that by making an enemy of Catharine Beecher, Woodhull had also become a target of Isabella's two other sisters, Harriet Beecher Stowe and Mary Beecher Perkins.

The Beecher sisters soon began investigating Victoria Woodhull's personal life in order to discredit her and her free love ideology. They wrote Isabella letters slandering Woodhull. Isabella did not, in fact, support free love, and had told Woodhull so. She also believed that the controversies surrounding Woodhull made her an unsuitable ally for the suffrage movement. Yet, as she told Susan B. Anthony, "I am keeping quiet however – still praising and defending her though my sisters, all three... have nearly crazed me with letters imploring me to have nothing to do with her..."[25] When Hooker refused to cut ties with Woodhull, her sisters wrote to her husband, John Hooker, asking him to influence her. John's silence only further agitated the Beecher sisters. "My poor wandering sister Bell," Harriet wrote, "if only she had a sensible husband, she might be brought right but John ministers to the very poorest and weakest part of her nature."[26] Harriet even suggested that Isabella's loyalty to Woodhull was the result of demonic possession. Despite the increasing pressure from her sisters, however, Isabella refused to sever ties with Woodhull.

Historians have suggested that Isabella Beecher Hooker's continuous defense of Woodhull was based her vision of a teenaged Victoria marrying the drunken Canning Woodhull. She pitied Woodhull and lashed out at Harriet Beecher Stowe and Mary Beecher Perkins for their criticisms. Hooker pointed out that both women had alcoholic sons and accused them of having a double standard for defending their sons' actions but condemning a woman who had suffered at the hands of an alcoholic husband. Hypocrisy infuriated Hooker as much as it did her sisters, and she was not going to be silent while they attacked Woodhull.

Victoria Woodhull was not the victim that Hooker imagined, however, and she did not need defending. If anything, the Beecher sisters' attacks only made her more committed to holding Henry Ward Beecher accountable for adultery. In May 1871, Woodhull learned more details of Henry's affair. He had conducted an extramarital relationship with Elizabeth Tilton, a parishioner at Plymouth Church and the wife of Beecher's protégé, the minister Theodore Tilton. Elizabeth Tilton had ultimately confessed to her husband, but the scandal became messier when each of the Tiltons began confiding to friends about the affair. Eventually, the gossip made its way to Woodhull, who—with her suspicions about Beecher confirmed—published an article in the *New York World* advocating free love and including a thinly veiled description of Henry Ward Beecher and his affair. "I know of one man, a public teacher of eminence who lives in concubinage with the wife of another public teacher of almost equal eminence," Woodhull wrote. "I shall make it my business to analyze some of these lives and will take my chances in the matter of libel suits."[27]

Victoria Woodhull had not outed Henry Ward Beecher by name, but for those who knew the story of his affair, her reference was obvious. There were also rumors this affair was not Beecher's first. For Woodhull, the accusations against Henry Ward Beecher were about fighting hypocrisy. If the charges had not been about her brother, Catharine Beecher might have supported Woodhull's attack. She had certainly challenged Alexander McWhorter's character for his relationship with Delia Bacon. Adultery was a more serious charge than the one leveled against McWhorter. And yet, for the Beechers, Woodhull was a threat. Catharine Beecher would not—could not—see in her brother the moral hypocrisy that she had spent her career exposing in other ministers.

Opposing Victoria Woodhull became an obsession for Harriet Beecher Stowe and Catharine Beecher. Stowe caricatured Woodhull in the novel *My Wife and I*. The Woodhull-based character was name "Miss Audacia Dangyereyes" and was known for bullying men into buying her newspaper and for rejecting femininity in favor of masculine behavior. Meanwhile, Catharine slandered Woodhull to anyone who would listen. When she learned that Woodhull was scheduled to speak in Hartford in November 1871, she wrote to the governor asking that he ban the speech. When he refused, she published an article in the newspaper denouncing free love and asking that Christian people refuse to discuss it in public. "… just now my sister Catharine is attacking Mrs. W[oodhull]'s private character *infamously* so as to keep people from going out to hear her [lecture]…" Isabella Beecher Hooker recounted. She was discouraged by her sisters' campaign against Woodhull, noting "it is dreadful this having foes in your own household…"[28] But Hooker did not abandon Woodhull simply because her sisters told her to. She predicted that Catharine's plan to foil Woodhull's speech would ultimately fail, and it did. Seven hundred people attended Woodhull's speech in Hartford, and, in it, Woodhull mocked Catharine Beecher's letter. She hoped, she said, to be a better Christian than Beecher. Beecher did not publicly respond to Woodhull's lecture, but she must have felt validated in her criticisms as Victoria Woodhull's infamy grew.

In 1872, Woodhull ran for president, even though women could not vote. As if her candidacy was not controversial enough, she announced that the former abolitionist Frederick Douglass would serve as her vice president, a fact that Douglass learned from newspapers. Her political bid went nowhere, however, and only further damaged her social standing. Among suffragists, only Isabella Beecher Hooker showed any support for Woodhull, and even she had private doubts about whether running for president was reasonable. By this time, Woodhull's patron, Cornelius Vanderbilt, had withdrawn his financial support. When Woodhull was evicted from her home, she was unable to find new lodging in a respectable area because of her reputation. That fall, when Plymouth Church hosted a twenty-fifth anniversary celebration to commemorate Henry Ward Beecher's tenure as minister, Woodhull had had enough. She decided to tell the country what she knew.

On October 28, 1872, Victoria Woodhull published an article entitled "The Beecher-Tilton Scandal Case" in *Woodhull and Claflin's Weekly*. Woodhull described the details of the affair and the attempts to cover it up. Within days, 150,000 copies of the issue had been sold. Typically, an issue of *Woodhull and Claflin's Weekly* cost $0.10. For this issue, people were paying as much as $20. The story became even more sensational when Woodhull and Tennessee Claflin were arrested for publishing obscenity. Harriet Beecher Stowe snidely called them "jailbirds." When she later learned that Woodhull and Claflin would be delivering a public speech in Boston, Stowe noted "The impudence of those witches is incredible!"[29] Neither the arrest of Woodhull and Claflin nor the Beecher's siblings defense of Henry could shield him from the fall out, however.

For Henry Ward Beecher, once "the idol of Brooklyn," being exposed as an adulterer was devastating.[30] He would spend the next few years fighting for his reputation in an ecclesiastical trial and a civil trial. These trials were some of the most sensational of the nineteenth-century. They began in 1873 when

Plymouth Church excommunicated Theodore Tilton for slandering Beecher. The next year the Congressional Church held a hearing to determine whether Plymouth Church had fully investigated Beecher before excommunicating Tilton. Plymouth Church then organized their own committee to investigate Beecher and that committee exonerated him. Theodore Tilton subsequently sued Henry Ward Beecher in civil court on the charges of adultery. This civil case, begun in 1875, ended seven months later. Jurors were unable to agree on a verdict. The following year the Congressional Church also cleared Beecher. For Henry Ward Beecher, the years that he dealt with the fall out of his affair with Elizabeth Tilton were miserable. He was in poor health and broke, having paid $180,000 (more than $4 million today) over the course of the trials. He had lost jobs as an essayist and editor of a journal. By 1877, however, he had landed back on his feet. His new career as a professional lecturer took him around the country, where people lined up to shake his hand and paid as much as $10 (more than $250 in modern currency) for standing room spots at his lectures. Whether it was his charisma, his famous name, or the privilege of being a White man, Henry Ward Beecher was able to rehabilitate his reputation. This was a privilege not afforded to Victoria Woodhull, who was impoverished after losing her brokerage firm and newspaper due to backlash from the Beecher-Tilton Affair.

The Beechers did not escape unscathed by Henry's scandal, however. Catharine noted that "One great difficulty in this scandal is the bitter malignity of forever warm friends..."[31] Harriet's relationship with Isabella was badly damaged. Catharine was more forgiving of her youngest sister but remained baffled by Isabella's dedication to the suffrage movement, writing "My soul is cast down at the ignorance and mistaken zeal of my poor sister Bell and her coagitators." She asked a friend,

> Can you not lend a helping pen to show what a mercy it is to woman *to have a head* to take the thousand responsibilities of family life—and how much *moral* power is gained by taking a subordinate place...[32]

After everything she had experienced, Catharine remained convinced that the key to women's power was the proper properly management of the domestic sphere. She told a friend, "I think the right training of women is now the chief problem of the age."[33]

Perhaps Catharine Beecher was motivated by a desire to help young women re-consider their place in society when she wrote her memoir *Educational Reminiscences and Suggestions*, published in 1874. The years had softened her viewpoint on the woman's right movement, but her conviction that her agenda for women was correct had not changed. She noted:

> ...while I deeply sympathized in the effort to remedy the many disabilities and sufferings of my sex, it seemed to me the most speedy and effective

remedy would be to train women for her true profession as educator and chief minister of the family state, and to secure to her the honor and pecuniary reward which men gain in their professions.[34]

She reasserted her dedication to female empowerment, but her arguments were as contradictory as ever. She stressed that women could be simultaneously submissive and independent. She attempted to resolve this paradox insisting that women's choice to be submissive somehow gave them autonomy. Many modern readers would find these ideas incompatible—Victoria Woodhull certainly challenged them. But Beecher wanted to offer women ways to assert themselves without upsetting the established gender roles. This memoir was Catharine Beecher's last publication.

At seventy-four years old, Catharine's health prohibited her from resuming the book tours and speaking engagements that had occupied her during middle age. And so, as she had throughout her life, she spent her final years living with her siblings. In 1877, Catharine moved in with her brother Thomas Beecher and his wife Julia in Elmira, New York. It was close to her favorite water-cure institute, the Gleason Sanitarium. "I am relieved and glad to think of you at home at last with brother Tom." Harriet Beecher Stowe wrote Beecher. "Too many years have passed over your head for you to be wandering like a trunk without a label." Beecher, however, still hoped to find "something to do." After fifty years of teaching, writing, and traveling it must have been difficult for her to relax in her brother's home. Harriet tried to soothe her sister's anxieties writing, "Towards the close of life we must all learn the lesson to retire gracefully and to accept the fact that we can no more be leaders." She advised Catharine to focus on music and singing, visiting patients at the Gleason Sanitarium and "[making] life brighter around you." "Meanwhile," she told Beecher, "the government of the world will not be going on a whit worse that *you* are not doing it..."[35] She had had a long career, and Stowe wanted her to relax.

Beecher was reluctant to fully retire, however. In April 1878, she wrote to her sister, Mary Beecher Perkins, that she had been going through her personal papers and was reminiscing about their youth. She missed charitable work. And yet, she told Perkins, she was comfortable in Thomas Beecher's home. She confided to Mary that she was prepared for the end of her life because—as John recounted of Jesus—she had "'finished the work my Father gave me to do.'"[36] Yet, despite the peace of mind Beecher had acquired, she was not entirely without ambition. Around the same time that she penned this letter, she began writing to publishers about a new project. She wanted, she wrote, for public schools to do more to educate women. In May, she wrote to the heads of schools in Philadelphia and New Jersey about forming a women's committee to discuss female education. Her passion, as always, was to ensure that women's education was equal to men's. This new project would never be realized, however, for on May 10, 1878, Catharine Beecher suffered a stroke. She died two days later without gaining consciousness. In a tribute to Beecher, one newspaper noted "Her life shows how much can be done by a hopeful, industrious mind."[37] "'There is no state,'" Henry Ward Beecher noted, "'where there are teachers who do not look up to her.'"[38] Catharine Beecher had indeed made her mark on the cultural history of the United States.

Notes

1. Catharine Beecher, *Common Sense Applied to Religion; or, The Bible and the People* (New York: Harper & Brothers, 1857), xviii.
2. C. Beecher, *Common Sense Applied to Religion*, 34.
3. Milton Rugoff, *The Beechers: An American Family in the Nineteenth Century* (New York: Harper and Row, 1981), 389.
4. Rugoff, 390.
5. Barbara A. White, *The Beecher Sisters* (New Haven: Yale University Press, 2003), 93.
6. Joan D. Hedrick, *Harriet Beecher Stowe: A Life* (New York: Oxford University Press, 1994), Location 5236. Kindle.
7. Catharine Beecher, *Religious Training of Children in the School, the Family, and the Church* (New York: Harper & Brothers, 1864), 220–221.
8. C. Beecher, *Religious Training*, 221.
9. Kathryn Kish Sklar, *Catharine Beecher: A Study in American Domesticity* (New York: W.W. Norton & Company, 1976), 255.
10. Rugoff, 360.
11. Catharine Beecher and Harriet Beecher Stowe, *The American Women's Home* (New York: J.B. Ford & Co., 1869), 19.
12. Sklar, 265.
13. Emma Gratia Hollister Royce. "My Personal Recollections of the Beecher Family," *Connecticut Historical Society*, 4.
14. Hedrick, 355.
15. Ibid.
16. Catharine E. Beecher to Elizabeth Cady Stanton, May 16, 1870, in *The Selected Papers of Elizabeth Cady Stanton and Susan B. Anthony, vol. II*, Ann D. Gordon, ed. (New Brunswick: Rutgers University Press, 1997), 335.
17. Mary Gabriel, *Notorious Victoria: The Uncensored Life of Victoria Woodhull——Visionary, Suffragist, and First Woman to Run for President* (Chapel Hill: Algonquin Books, 1998), Location 51. Kindle.
18. "The Washington Convention," *Woodhull and Claflin Weekly*, January 27, 1872, 5.
19. Debby Applegate, *The Most Famous Man in America: The Biography of Henry Ward Beecher* (New York: Doubleday Press, 2006), 412.
20. Victoria Woodhull, "Great Fight on the Woman Question," *Woodhull and Claflin Weekly*, January 14, 1871, 10.
21. Catharine Beecher, "A Word to the Ladies of New York," as reprinted in "The Beauties (Infamies) of Modern Journalism," *Woodhull and Claflin Weekly*, May 17, 1863, 15.
22. Applegate, 413.
23. "The Beauties (Infamies) of Modern Journalism," *Woodhull and Claflin Weekly*, May 17, 1863, 15.
24. Ida Husted Harper, *The Life and Work of Susan B. Anthony*, vol. 1 (e-art now, 2007), 440. Google Books. Originally published Indianapolis: The Bowen-Merril Company, 1899.
25. Jeanne Boydston, Mary Kelly, and Anne Margolis, *The Limits of Sisterhood: The Beecher Sisters on Women's Rights and Women's Sphere* (Chapel Hill: University of North Carolina Press, 1988), 206

26 White, 173.
27 Applegate, 414.
28 Boydston, et al., 313.
29 Boydston, et al., 289.
30 Emma Gratia Hollister Royce, "My Personal Recollections of the Beecher Family," *Connecticut Historical Society*, 1.
31 Catharine E. Beecher to the Editor of the *Tribune*, September 22, 1874, Henry Ward Beecher Papers, folder 2, The New York Public Library Manuscript and Archives Division.
32 Catharine Beecher to Leonard Bacon, March 9, 1872, in Jeanne Boydstron, et al., 257.
33 Ibid.
34 Catharine Beecher, *Educational Reminiscences and Suggestions* (New York: J.B. Ford and Company, 1874), 101.
35 Harriet Beecher Stowe to Catharine Beecher, n.d. in Jeanne Boydston, et al., 353–354.
36 Catharine Beecher to Mary Beecher Perkins, April 29, 1878, in Boydston, et al., 354.
37 "Catherine Beecher: Her Death Expected," *New York Herald*, May 11, 1878, 4.
38 "Catherine Beecher: Her Death Expected," 4.

EPILOGUE

Catharine Beecher's dedication to expanding education never wavered. In her 70s, she walked into the office of Dr. Andrew White, President of Cornell University, and announced her intention to take a course at the school. Embarrassed, White explained to her that Cornell was an exclusively male institution. "Oh, that is quite all right, Doctor White," Beecher replied, "in fact I prefer to take [courses] with men." When White offered to help her find lodging in town, she once again surprised him by explaining that she would be living in the dormitory. "But, Miss Beecher," he said, "that is a dormitory for young men, it has no accommodations for ladies!" She replied, "I have inspected the accommodations and find them entirely satisfactory and as for those young men, who are of appropriate ages to be my grandsons, they will not trouble me in the least."[1] She lived in the dormitory for the term and took the course.

Beecher's request to study with men may have shocked Dr. White, but for her it was in line with a lifelong contention that women were entitled to the same education as men. As an educator, herself, she had pushed women's education away from the ornamental branches of study, such as dancing and sewing, and focused it instead on mathematics, science, and physical education. And yet, she remained conservative in critical ways. She insisted throughout her life that women's gender differences were a strength that would be undermined by complete gender equality. Beecher also largely ignored racial issues. Her dedication to education did not extend to people of color, even after the Civil War. For most of her life, Beecher scoffed at women's suffrage, arguing that women's greatest influence would not be in politics as the Grimke sisters and woman's suffragists believed, but in the home. On this point her views did not change, but rather evolved from the ideology of Republican Motherhood, which had shaped her youth, to her own point that domesticity was a science. Beecher's arguments remained focused on empowering women to approach their roles as wives, mothers, and teachers as professions. These ideas would be crucial to her role in promoting the nineteenth-century cult of domesticity.

And yet while Beecher fostered the image of the ideal woman in her writings, she did not fully embody that woman, herself. Her life was full of contradictions. She never married or had children though she elevated domestic life in her writing. As a career woman, she was not satisfied taking a submissive role to men. Her personality was at times nurturing, at others demanding. She wrote books on health yet was often incapacitated by illness. Her students and protégées adored her, but her siblings found her judgmental and difficult. In studying Catharine Beecher, it is important to accept these contradictions for she was ever the self-promoter and carefully curated what personal information she divulged in her writings. The paradoxes in Beecher's life also reflected the decades in which she lived. When she was born in 1800, the United States was largely a rural, agricultural nation. When she died in 1878, most Americans lived in cities and worked in factories. New territories spanned the entire continental United States and were linked by railroads, canals, and paved roads. Immigration had diversified the nation. Enslaved persons had been freed. White women had gained rights to own property after marriage and were campaigning for suffrage. Did Catharine Beecher struggle with these changes? It is difficult to say with any certainty. What is clear, is that as a young woman she dreamed of equal educational opportunities for women. As she aged, she fought passionately to protect their right to education and to install women as teachers with the same pay and job security as their male counterparts. In these crusades, Beecher both enjoyed success and suffered failure. Women's education did match the curricula offered to men, but female teaching jobs remained low paying and unstable. Beecher was frustrated and blamed powerful men, specifically the clergy for this professional inequality. And herein was another contradiction. The flaws that she was so willing to expose in ministers, she struggled to acknowledge in her own male family members. In many ways, Catharine's loyalties were to the Beechers first and to women second. These conflicts reveal that she struggled to understand her own position just as we struggle to understand her today. Nevertheless, Beecher's argument about the importance of gender differences serves as a legacy for conservative women throughout the twenty-first century as they shape their understanding of their roles in society.

In recent years television personalities like Martha Stewart, Oprah Winfrey, and Joanna Gaines have built careers from offering domestic advice. Yet—like Beecher—they do this from the perspective of career women. Stewart's brand "Martha Stewart Living" markets home furnishings ranging from furniture to paint. The associated magazine offers advice on household tasks from baking to health and does so by emphasizing the importance of domesticity. Similarly, Winfrey's magazine *O, The Oprah Magazine* provides recipes and advice on health and beauty. Gaines celebrates the restorative power of the home on the television network, Magnolia, which she co-owns with her husband Chip. These women are our modern domestic advisers and they, like Beecher exalt the home and its comforts. *Treatise of Domestic Economy* may no longer be read by women looking for household tips, but Catharine Beecher's influence is still everywhere.

Note

1 Lyman Beecher Stowe, *Saints, Sinners and Beechers* (Indianapolis: The Bobbs-Merrill Company, 1933), 129–130.

PRIMARY SOURCES

Excerpt from letter from Catharine Beecher to Lyman Beecher, 1823

When I think of Mr. Fisher, and remember his blameless and useful life, his unexampled and persevering efforts to do his duty to both God and man, I believe that a merciful Savior has not left him to perish at last; that if He had delayed an answer to his supplications till the last sad hour; it was then bestowed; and that, in the Day of Judgment we shall find that God is influenced in bestowing his grace by the efforts of men; that He does make the needful distinctions between virtue and vice; and that there was more reason to hope for one whose life had been an example of excellence, than for one who had spent his days in guilt and sin.

Circular Addressed to the Benevolent Ladies of the United States *by Catharine Beecher, 1829*

As we have risen to greatness and glory, the Indian nations have faded away. Their proud and powerful tribes are gone, their noble sachems and mighty warriors are heard of no more, and it is said the Indian often comes to the borders of his limited retreat to gaze on the beautiful country no longer his own, and to cry with bitterness at the remembrance of past greatness and power.

Ever since the existence of this nation, our general government, pursing the course alike of policy and benevolence, have acknowledged these people as free and independent nations, and has protected them in the quiet possession of their lands. In repeated treaties with the Indians, the United States, by the hands of the most distinguished statesman, after purchasing the greater part of their best lands, have *promised* them *"to continue the guaranty of the remainder of their country FOREVER."* And so strictly has government guarded the Indian's right to his lands, that even to go on to their boundaries to survey the land. subjects [one] to heavy fines and imprisonment ...

But they are beginning to be oppressed and threatened, and when they have looked for protection and help, it has been refused. Already we begin to hear them lamenting, that they, must leave their country, the land of their fathers, and all that is dearest to them on earth ..

Have not the females of the country some duties devolving upon them in retaliation to this helpless race? They are protected from the blinding influence of party spirit, and aspirates of political violence. They have nothing to do with any struggle for power nor any right to dictate the decisions of those that rule over them.

Excerpt from *An Appeal to the Christian Women of the South* by Angelina Grimke, 16–17

But perhaps you will be ready to query, why appeal to *women* on this subject? We do not make the laws which perpetuate slavery. No legislative power is vested in us; *we* can do nothing to overthrow the system, even if we wished to do so. To this I reply, I know you do not make the laws, but I also know that you *are the wives and mothers, the sisters and daughters of those who do*; and if you really suppose you can do nothing to overthrow slavery, you are greatly mistaken. You can do much in every way: four things I will name... You can read on the subject. 2d. You can pray over this subject. 3d. You can speak on this subject. 4th. You can *act* on this subject. I have not placed reading before praying because I regard it more important, but because, in order to pray aright, we must understand what we are praying for; it is only then we can "pray with understanding, and the spirit also.

Excerpt from *An Essay on Slavery and Abolition, with References to the Duty of American Females* by Catharine Beecher, 1837, 100–102

Addressed to Miss A.D. Grimke

My Dear Friend,

Your public address to Christian females at the South has reached me, and I have been urged to aid in circulating it at the North. I have also been informed, that you contemplate a tour, during the ensuing year, for the purpose of exerting your influences to form Abolitionist Societies among ladies of the non-slaveholding States.

Our acquaintance and friendship give me claim to your private ear; but there are reasons why it seems more desirable to address you, who now stand before the public as an advocate of Abolitionist measures, in a more public manner...

It is Christianity that has given to woman her true place in society. And it is that peculiar trait of Christianity alone that can sustain her therein. "Peace on earth and good will to men" is the character of all the rights and privileges, the influence, and the power of woman. A man may act on society by the collision of intellect, in public debate; he may urge his measures by a sense of shame, by fear and by personal interest; he may coerce by the combination of public sentiment; he may drive by physical force, and does not outstep the boundaries of his sphere. But all the power, and all the conquests that are lawful to woman, are those only which appeal to the kindly, generous, peaceful and benevolent principles.

Woman is to win everything by peace and love; by making herself so much respected, esteemed and loved, that to yield to her opinions and to gratify her wishes, will be the free-will offering of the heart. But this is to be all accomplished in the domestic and social circle. There let every woman become so cultivated and refined in intellect, that her taste and judgment will be respected; so benevolent in feeling and action; that her motives will be reverenced;—so unassuming and unambitious, that collision and competition be banished;—so "gentle and easy to be entreated," as that every heart will repose in her presence; then, the fathers, the husbands, and the sons, will find an influence thrown around them, to which they will yield not only willingly but proudly. A man is never ashamed to own such influences, but feels dignified and ennobled in acknowledging them. But the moment woman begins to feel the promptings of ambition, or the thirst for power, her aegis of defence (*sic*) is gone. All the sacred protection of religion, all the generous promptings of chivalry, all the poetry of romantic gallantry, depend on woman's retaining her place as dependent and defenceless (*sic*), and making no claims, and maintaining no right but what are the gifts of honour (*sic*), rectitude, and love.

Excerpt from *Letters to Catharine E. Beecher, In Reply to An Essay on Slavery and Abolitionism, Addressed to A.E. Grimke*, 103–105

Dear Friend:

I come now to that part of thy book, which is, of all others, the most important to the women of this country; thy 'general views in relation to the place woman is appointed to fill by the dispensations of heaven.' I shall quote paragraphs from thy book, offer my objections to them, and then throw before thee my own views…

'Woman is to win everything by peace and love; by making *herself* so much respected, &c. that to yield to *her* opinions, and to gratify *her* wishes, will be the free-will offering of the heart.' This principle may do as the rule of action to the fashionable belle, whose idol is *herself*, whose every attitude and smile are designed to win the admiration of others to *herself* and who enjoys, with exquisite delight, the double-refined incense of flattery, which is offered to *her* vanity, by yielding to *her* opinions, and gratifying *her* wishes, because they are *hers*. But to the humble Christian, who feels that it is *truth* which she seeks to recommend to others, *truth* which she wants them to esteem and love, and not herself, this subtle principle must be rejected with holy indignation. Suppose she could win thousands to her opinions, and govern them by her wishes, how much nearer would they be to Jesus Christ, if she presents no higher motive, and points to no higher leader?

Excerpt from *Treatise on Domestic Economy*, 1841 by Catharine Beecher, 3

The tendencies of democratic institutions, in reference to the rights and interests of the female sex, have been fully developed in the United States; and it is in this aspect, that the subject is one of peculiar interest to American women. In this country, it is established, both by opinion and by practice, that woman has an equal interest in all social and civil concerns; and that no domestic, civil, or political, institution, is right, which sacrifices her interest to promote that of the other sex. But in order to secure her the more firmly in all these privileges, it is decided, that, in the domestic relation, she take a subordinate station, and that, in civil and political concerns, her interests be entrusted to the other sex, without her taking any part in voting or in making and administering laws.

Excerpt from *Letters to the People on Health and Happiness* by Catharine Beecher, 1851, 103–104

As to exercise, the whole of childhood and youth, up to eighteen, was one long play-spell out of doors. In those days the "higher branches" had not invaded the school room for girls.[1] A quick and retentive memory secured all the lessons required in less than an hour of daily study, and a kindly teacher and easy parents looked with forbearance on school-hours spent in roving over hill and dale, and in concocting plays and jokes.

The result was that I can not *(sic)* recall the memory of a single day of sickness from infancy to the age of twenty. True, sometimes a cold was caught and an anxious and tender father, on such occasions, would always summon the wise and good physician, known all over the STATE for his *great success and few doses*...[2]

...All the memories of my youth are those of *perfect* health, and that physical and mental enjoyment that are its natural attendance. Such was the result on a mind constitutionally a cheerful one, that the greatest trouble to me and to my parents was, that I was too happy and too merry to be able to think long of anything solemn, or to fear any evil in this world or the other.

But when womanhood came, then I must earn my own livelihood. And so, after a period of preparation that shut me up in the house, I started as a teacher of music and painting, and thus was confined in the house to breathe such as most young girls are condemned to inspire through all their school-life, generally both by night and day, especially at boarding-schools. In less than two years the weak eyes and cutaneous affections of infancy returned, proving that it was pure air and outdoor exercise that had protected me from them all through my childhood and youth.

Excerpt from *Woman's Profession as Mother and Educator, with Views in Opposition to Woman Suffrage* by Catharine Beecher, 194–195

Another evil to be apprehended from introducing women into political life is increasing the temptations to draw them from the humble, self-sacrificing Christian labor among the ignorant and neglected, which now is so imperfectly supplied. To be a member of the Legislature, a member of Congress, a Judge, a Governor, or a President, are temptations heretofore unknown to women. Who shall we say what would be the result should every woman of *every class in society* be stimulated by such temptations?

Notes

1 Beecher is referencing the fact that girl's schools did not teach mathematics or science.
2 "Few doses" refers to the doctor's choice to not administer medicine.—

STUDY QUESTIONS

1. Based on this letter, how did Alexander Fisher's death shape Catharine Beecher's religious views?
2. How does Catharine Beecher describe indigenous people? What does *Circular* reveal about women's political participation during the 1820s?
3. In *Circular*, how does Beecher recommend that women defend Native Americans?
4. How do Catharine Beecher's life experiences illuminate the challenges faced by nineteenth-century women? In what ways was Beecher's own life a contradiction?
5. Based on the primary sources, what does Beecher argue is the role of women in society?
6. What is the cult of domesticity? Does Catharine Beecher exemplify this ideal?
7. How did Catharine Beecher's viewpoints mesh with the rest of the Beecher family?
8. What are the major points of contention between Angelina Grimke and Catharine Beecher? How do these disagreements demonstrate the larger argument between conservative and radical reformers?
9. According to *Treatise on Domestic Economy*, how does Catharine Beecher see women participating in democracy?
10. What purpose does Beecher's personal story serve in *Letters to the People in Health and Happiness*?
11. Why does Beecher see woman's suffrage as a danger to society?
12. Do Catharine Beecher's ideas relate to our modern ideas about gender? Why or why not?

BIBLIOGRAPHY

Primary Sources

Books

Acts Passed at a General Assembly of the Commonwealth of Virginia. Richmond: Thomas Richie, 1833.

Beecher, Catharine. *An Essay on the Education of Female Teachers, for the United States* in Shirley Nelson Kersey, *Classics in the Education of Girls and Women*. Metuchen, NJ: Scarecrow Press, 1981.

———. *An Essay on Slavery and Abolitionism*. Philadelphia: Henry Perkins, 1837.

———. *Common Sense Applied to Religion; or, The Bible and the People*. New York: Harper & Brothers, 1857.

———. *Educational Reminiscences and Suggestions*. New York: J.B. Ford and Company, 1874.

———. *Letters to the People on Health and Happiness*. New York: Harper & Brothers Publishers, 1855.

———. *Physiology and Calisthenics for Schools and Families*. New York: Harper & Brothers, 1856.

———. *Religious Training of Children in the School, the Family, and the Church*. New York: Harper & Brothers, 1864.

———. *Suggestions Respecting Improvements in Education, Presented to the Trustees of the Hartford Female Seminary*. Hartford: Packard and Butler, 1829.

———. *The Elements of Mental and Moral Philosophy, Founded Upon Experience, Reason and the Bible*. Hartford, 1831.

———. *The Evils Suffered by American Women and American Children: The Causes and Remedy*. New York: Harper and Brothers, 1847.

———. *The True Remedy for the Wrongs of Women with a History of An Enterprise Having that for Its Object*. Boston: Philips, Sampson & Co., 1851.

———. *Treatise on Domestic Economy for the use of Young Ladies at Home and at School.* New York: Harper & Brothers Publishers, 1849.

———. *Truth Stranger Than Fiction: A Narrative of Recent Transactions, Involving Enquiries in Regard to the Principles of Honor, Truth, and Justice, Which Obtain in a Distinguished American University.* Boston: Phillips, Sampson & Co., 1850.

Beecher, Catharine and Harriet Beecher Stowe. *The American Women's Home.* New York: J.B. Ford & Co., 1869.

Beecher, Lyman. *A Plea for the West.* Cincinnati: Truman and Smith, 1835.

———. *Autobiography, Correspondence, Etc., of Lyman Beecher,* vol. I. Edited by Charles Beecher. London: S. Low, Son and Marston, 1863.

———. *Autobiography, Correspondence, Etc., of Lyman Beecher,* vol. II. Edited by Charles Beecher. New York: Harper & Brothers Publishers, 1865.

Chestnut, Mary. *Mary Chestnut's Civil War.* Edited by C. Vann Woodward. New Haven: Yale University Press, 1981.

"Declaration of Sentiments" in Jean Matthews *Women's Struggle for Equality: The First Phase, 1828–1876.* Chicago: Ivan R. Dee, 1997.

Grimke, Angelina. *Appeal to the Christian Women of the South.* New York: American Anti-Slavery Society, 1836.

———. *Letters to Catharine Beecher, In Reply to an Essay on Slavery and Abolitionism, Addressed to A.E. Grimke Revised by Author, Letter XII Human Rights Not Founded on Sex.* Boston: Isaac Knapp, 1838a.

———. *Letters to Catharine Beecher,* "Slavery and the Boston riot. The following letter was written, shortly after the pro-slavery riot in Boston by Angeline E. Grimke to William Lloyd Garrison... 1835. Boston: 1835." Library of Congress, Rare Book and Special Collections Division, Printed Ephemera Collection.

Grimke, Sarah. *Letters on the Equality of the Sexes.* Boston: Isaac Knapp, 1838b.

Murray, Judith Sargent. "The Gleaner Contemplates the Future Prospects of Women in this 'Enlightened Age'," 125–129 in Shelia L. Skemp, ed. *Judith Sargent Murray: A Brief Biography with Documents.* New York: Bedford/St. Martin's, 1998.

Nichols, Mary Gove. *Experiences in Water-Cure.* New York: Fowler and Wells, 1852.

Norton, Minerva Brace. *A True Teacher: Mary Mortimer, a Memoir.* New York: Fleming H. Revell Company, 1894.

[Unknown]. "Reminiscences of Alexander Metcalf Fisher, late Professor of Mathematics and Natural Philosophy in Yale College." *New Englander and Yale Review* 1:4 (October 1843): 457–469.

Sklar, Kathryn Kish, ed. *Women's Rights Emerges within the Anti-Slavery Movement, 1830–1870: A Brief History with Documents.* New York: Palgrave MacMillan, 2000.

Stowe, Charles Edward. *The Life of Harriet Beecher Stowe: Compiled from Her Letters and Journals.* Boston: Houghton, Mifflin, and Company, 1890.

Stowe, Harriet Beecher. *Life and Letters of Harriet Beecher Stowe.* Edited by Annie Fields. Cambridge: Riverside Press, 1897.

———. *Oldtown Folks.* Boston: Fields, Osgood & Co., 1869.

The Selected Papers of Elizabeth Cady Stanton and Susan B. Anthony, vol. II. Edited by Ann D. Gordon. New Brunswick: Rutgers University Press, 1997.

Van Buren, Martin. *The Autobiography of Martin Van Buren.* Edited by John C Fitzpatrick. Washington: Government Printing Officer, 1920.

Manuscripts

Adams Family Papers, *Founders Online*, National Archives. https://founders.archives.gov/documents/Adams/04-02-02-0058.
Henry Ward Beecher Papers. New York Public Library.
Johnson Family Papers, Connecticut Historical Society.
Royce, Emma Gratia Hollister. "My Personal Recollections of the Beecher Family," Connecticut Historical Society.

Newspapers

Lewis' New Gymnastics for Ladies, Gentleman and Children and the Boston Journal of Physical Culture
New York Herald
New York Times
Peterson's Magazine
Woodhull and Claflin Weekly

Secondary Sources

Journal Articles

Hershberger, Mary. "Mobilizing Women, Anticipating Abolition: The Struggle Against Indian Removal in the 1830s." *The Journal of American History* 86:1 (June 1999): 15–40.
Jakle, John A. "Cincinnati in the 1830s: A Cognitive Map of Traveler's Landscape Impressions." *Environmental Review* 3:2 (Spring 1979): 2–10.
Theodore, Alisse. "'A Right to Speak on the Subject': The US Women's Antiremoval Petition Campaign, 1829–1831." *Rhetoric and Public Affairs* 5:4 (Winter 2002): 601–623.

Chapters in Edited Collections

Ogren, Christine A. "Betrothed to the State?: Nineteenth-Century Academies Confront the Rise of the State Normal Schools," 284–303 in *Chartered Schools: Two Hundred Years of Independent Academies, 1727–1925*. Edited by Nancy Beadie and Kim Tolley. New York: Routledge Falmer Press, 2002.
Terzian, Sevan G. and Nancy Beadie, "'Let the People Remember It': Academies and the Rise of Public High Schools, 1865–1890," in *Chartered Schools: Two Hundred Years of Independent Academies, 1727–1925*. Edited by Nancy Beadie and Kim Tolley. New York: Routledge Falmer Press, 2002.
Tolley, Kim. "Mapping the Landscape of Higher Schooling, 1727–1850," in *Chartered Schools: Two Hundred Years of Independent Academies in the United States, 1727–1925*. Edited by Nancy Beadie and Kim Tolley. New York: Routledge Falmer, 2002.

Books

Applegate, Debby. *The Most Famous Man in America: The Biography of Henry Ward Beecher*. New York: Doubleday Press, 2006.
Berkin, Carol. *Civil War Wives: The Lives and Times of Angelina Grimke Weld, Varina Howell Davis, & Julia Dent Grant*. New York: Vintage Books, 2009.

Blumin, Stuart M. *The Emergence of the Middle Class: Social Experience in the American City, 1760–1900.* New York: Cambridge University Press, 1989.

Boydston, Jeanne. *Home and Work: Housework, Wages and the Ideology of Labor in the Early Republic.* New York: Oxford University Press, 1990.

Boydston, Jeanne, Mary Kelly, and Anne Margolis. *The Limits of Sisterhood: The Beecher Sisters on Women's Rights and Women's Sphere.* Chapel Hill: University of North Carolina Press, 1988.

Cayleff, Susan E. *Wash and Be Healed: The Water-Cure Movement and Women's Health.* Philadelphia: Temple University Press, 1987.

Cott, Nancy F. *Public Vows: A History of Marriage and the Nation.* Cambridge: Harvard University Press, 2000.

Frawley, Maria H. *Invalidism and Identity in Nineteenth-Century Britain.* Chicago: University of Chicago Press, 2004.

Gabriel, Mary. *Notorious Victoria: The Uncensored Life of Victoria Woodhull—Visionary, Suffragist, and First Woman to Run for President.* Chapel Hill: Algonquin Books, 1998. Kindle.

Ginzberg, Lori. *Elizabeth Cady Stanton: An American Life.* New York: Hill and Wang, 2010.

———. *Women and the Work of Benevolence: Morality, Politics, and Class in the Nineteenth-Century United States.* New Haven: Yale University Press, 1990.

Hedrick, Joan D. *Harriet Beecher Stowe: A Life.* New York: Oxford University Press, 1994. Kindle.

Howe, Daniel Walker. *What Hath God Wrought: The Transformation of America, 1815–1848.* New York: Oxford University Press, 2007.

Johnston, Carolyn Ross. *Cherokee Women in Crisis: Trail of Tears, Civil War, and Allotment, 1838–1907.* Tuscaloosa: University of Alabama Press, 2003.

Kaestle, Carl F. *Pillars of the Republic.* New York: Hill and Wang, 1983.

Kelley, Mary. *Learning to Stand and Speak: Women, Education, and Public Life in America's Republic.* Chapel Hill: University of Carolina Press, 2014.

Kerber, Linda. *No Constitutional Right to be Ladies: Women and the Obligations of Citizenship.* New York: Hill and Wang, 1999.

Leavitt, Sarah A. *From Catharine Beecher to Martha Stewart: A Cultural History of Domestic Advice.* Chapel Hill: The University of North Carolina Press, 2002.

Lesick, Lawrence Thomas. *The Lane Rebels: Evangelicalism and Antislavery in Antebellum America.* Metuchen, NJ: Scarecrow Press, 1980.

Manion, Jen. *Female Husbands: A Trans History.* New York: Cambridge University Press, 2020.

Matthews, Jean. *Women's Struggle for Equality: The First Phase, 1828–1876.* Chicago: Ivan R. Dee, 1997.

Nash, Margaret. *Women's Education in the United States, 1780–1840.* New York: Palgrave Macmillan, 2005.

Rugoff, Milton. *The Beechers: An American Family in the Nineteenth-Century.* New York: Harper & Row Publishers, 1981.

Sears, Clare. *Arresting Dress: Cross-Dressing, Law, and Fascination in Nineteenth-Century San Francisco.* Durham: Duke University Press, 2015.

Sklar, Kathryn Kish. *Catharine Beecher: A Study in American Domesticity.* New York: W.W. Norton & Company, 1976.

Stansell, Christine. *City of Women: Sex and Class in New York 1789–1860.* Urbana: University of Illinois Press, 1987

Starr, Paul. *The Social Transformation of American Medicine: The Rise of a Sovereign Profession and the Making of a Vast Industry*. New York: Basic Books, 1982.

Taylor, Nikki M. *Frontiers of Freedom: Cincinnati's Black Community, 1802–1868*. Athens: University of Ohio Press, 2005.

Todd, Jan. *Physical Culture and the Body Beautiful: Purposive Exercise in the Lives of American Women, 1800–1875*. Macon: Mercer University Press, 1999.

Trotter, Joe William. *River Jordan: African American Urban Life in the Ohio Valley*. Lexington: University of Kentucky Press, 1998.

White, Barbara A. *The Beecher Sisters*. New Haven: Yale University Press, 2003.

INDEX

abolition/abolitionist/abolitionism 2–4, 33–37, 46–54, 71–73, 92–95, 100–101, 103, 105, 112; *see also* anti-slavery
American Colonization Society 37, 46; *see also* colonizationists
American Woman's Education Association 85
American Revolution 5–6, 10, 18, 19, 28, 30, 44, 55
Anthony, Susan B. 71, 105–106, 108, 110
anti-abolition 34–36, 48, 52
anti-slavery 1, 3, 6, 33–37, 46, 48–52, 71–72, 99–100; *see also* abolition

Bacon, Delia 75–77, 80, 83, 111
Beecher, Catharine: *American Woman's Home* 103; *An Appeal to the People on Behalf of Their Rights as Authorized Interpreters of the Bible*; *Religious Training of Children in the School, the Family, and the Church* 98; *An Essay on the Education of Female Teachers, for the United States* 32; anti-abolitionist stance 47, 49–55; Anti-sixteenth Amendment Society 106, 108; childhood 8–14; "Circular Addressed to the Benevolent Ladies of the United States," 45; Cincinnati, Catharine Beecher in 3, 27–33, 36–39, 61, 67, 78, 91; *Common Sense Applied to Religion, or the Bible and the People* 98; conservativism 41, 46, 50–55; conversion to Episcopal Church 99; *Domestic Receipt Book* 69; *Duty of American Women* 92; *Educational Reminiscences and Suggestions* 113; *Essay on Slavery and Abolitionism, with Reference to the Duty of American Females* 50–51; fame 65, 67; fundraising 23, 31, 33, 45, 67–69, 70, 78–79, 83, 85–86, 88, 105; Hartford, Catharine Beecher in 3, 16, 18, 22–26, 29, 33, 38, 45–46, 76, 84, 94, 103, 106, 112; *Letters on the Difficulties of Religion* 62; *Letters to the People on Health and Happiness* 85, 86–88; Litchfield, Catharine Beecher in 8, 10–11, 14, 29, 38; *see also* Litchfield Female Academy; Milwaukee, Catharine Beecher in 3, 81–85, 90, 98, 103; *see also* Milwaukee Female Institute; opposition to woman's suffrage 3–4, 32, 106, 109, 113, 117; *see also* Catharine Beecher: Anti-Sixteenth Amendment Society; *Physiology and Calisthenics for Schools and Families* 88–89; relationship with Alexander Metcalf Fisher 14–15; religious doubts 15–16; semi-colon club 30; Student at Litchfield Female Academy 11, 14, 89; *see also* Litchfield Female Academy; Sarah Pierce; *The Evils Suffered by American Women: The Causes and the Remedy* 68; *The Moral Instructor for Schools and Families:*

Containing Lessons on the Duties of Life, Arranged for Study and Recitation, Also Designed as a Reading Book for Schools 62; *Treatise on Domestic Economy, For the Use of Young Ladies at Home and at School* 55, 57, 62, 65, 67, 69, 75, 88, 103; *True Remedy for the Wrongs of Women* 84–85, 91; *Truth Stranger Than Fiction* 77; *Woman's Profession as Mother and Educator with Views in Opposition to Woman Suffrage* 107
Beecher, Edward 15–16, 22–23, 26, 36
Beecher, Harriet Porter 12–13, 84
Beecher, Henry Ward: abolitionism 95; accusations made by Victoria Woodhull 110–111; American Woman Suffrage Association 106
Beecher's Bibles 94
Beecher-Tilton Affair 111–113
Bleeding Kansas 94; Civil War 99–101
Plymouth Church 1, 94, 111–113
Reconstruction 102–103
Beecher, Lydia Beals Jackson 84–85
Beecher, Lyman: *A Plea for the West* 32, 38; religion 15, 38; death 100; minister in East Hampton 5–10; minister in Litchfield 10–11, 101; president of Lane Theological Seminary 26, 33, 36–37, 62; relationship with Catharine Beecher 5, 9–10, 84–85, 98
Beecher, Roxana Foote 6–13, 58; death 12
Beecher, Thomas 100, 114
Black male suffrage 103, 105
Bleeding Kansas 94–95
Brown, John 95
Burlington, Iowa 79–80, 82

calisthenics 4, 23–24, 88–89; *see also* Catharine Beecher: *Physiology and Calisthenics for Schools and Families*
Calvinist/Calvinism/Calvinistic 7, 15–16, 99
Central Committee for Promoting National Education 67, 69; *see also* National Board of Popular Education
The Civil War 2–3, 30–31, 72, 94, 99–102, 105, 108, 117
college plan 79–80, 82–83
colonization/colonizationists 35–37, 46–48, 52; *see also* American Colonization Society
common schools 20–21, 70
Compromise of 1850 93–94

conversion (religious) 7, 13, 15, 16, 76
corsets 4, 85–86
coverture *see* feme covert status
cult of domesticity 59–61, 109, 118; *see also* true womanhood

Declaration of Sentiments 73; *see also* Woman's Rights Movement
domestic economy 57, 61, 70, 74, 84–85, 90
domestic medicine 64, 88
Douglass, Frederick 46, 105, 112
Dred Scott Decision 95
Dutton, Mary 31, 39

education: after the American Revolution 18–21; during the nineteenth-century 21–22; *see also* Hartford Female Seminary: curriculum; reform 25, 31, 67–69, 73–74; *see also* Hartford Female Seminary: curriculum; college plan
Emancipation Proclamation 100

female hysteria 74
feme covert status/coverture 7, 59
Fisher, Alexander Metcalf 14–16
Fifteenth-Amendment 102, 105
Fourteenth-Amendment 102, 105

Garrison, William Lloyd 33, 46, 48–49, 71
Grimke, Angelina: abolition 4, 47–49, 51; *Appeal to the Christian Women of the South* 49; debate with Catharine Beecher 50–55
Grimke, Sarah: abolition 4, 47–48, 51; *Letters on the Equality of the Sexes, and the Condition of Women* 54, 73

Hartford Female Seminary: curriculum 22–26, 89; fundraising 23; reopening 104–105
heroic medicine 64, 75
Hooker, Isabella Beecher 2, 75, 90–92, 100–101, 105–106, 109–112

Immigration/immigrants 2, 31–34, 70, 74, 82, 93, 103, 118; *see also* Irish
Indian Removal/Indian Removal Act 41, 43–45, 49–50
Irish 34, 59–60, 69

Jackson, Andrew 41, 43–44, 45
Johnson, Nancy 75, 77–80, 83

Kansas-Nebraska Act 95

Lane Rebels 37, 62
Lane Theological Seminary 26, 29, 33, 36, 62; *see also* Lyman Beecher.
Lincoln, Abraham 94–95, 99–102
Litchfield Female Academy 10, 25; curriculum 11; physical education at 11
Lowell Mills 68–69, 73

Mann, Horace 69–70
Market Revolution 10, 41, 64
The Mexican War 93
Milwaukee Female Institute 83–86, 88, 90, 98
Missouri Compromise 93–94
moral education 24–25
moral training 24–26, 70
Mortimer, Mary 83–84
Mott, Lucretia 46, 51, 71–72
movement cure 85–86, 89

Nat Turner Rebellion 33–34
National Board of Popular Education 74, 80, 83; *see also* Central Committee for Promoting National Education.
Native Americans 2, 19, 32, 38, 41–46; *see also* Indian Removal/Indian Removal Act

Perkins, Mary Beecher 2, 110–111, 114
Physical Education 4, 11, 24, 86, 89, 117; *see also* Catharine Beecher: *Letters to the People on Health and Happiness*
Pierce, Sarah 10–11; *see also* Litchfield Female Academy
professionalization of teaching 70

Quincy, Illinois 79–80

Reconstruction 2–3, 102, 105
Republican Motherhood 8, 25, 70–71, 117

Second Great Awakening 3, 61, 71
Seneca Falls Convention 72–74; *see also* Declaration of Sentiments
separate spheres 59, 65, 71
Slade, William 70, 73–75, 77–80, 83
Stanton, Elizabeth Cady 71–72, 105–106, 108
Stone, Lucy 71, 105–106
Stowe, Calvin 36, 67–68, 70, 92, 100, 104, 106
Stowe, Harriet Beecher: abolition 36, 47, 95; during the Civil War 100; Hartford Female Seminary 31, 91, 104; memories of childhood 9–10, 12; on Abraham Lincoln 100, 102; on Victoria Woodhull 109–112; principal of Western Female Institute 31; Reconstruction 102–103; relationship with Catharine Beecher 9, 62, 91–92, 99, 103–104, 114; *Uncle Tom's Cabin* 1, 47, 91–94, 100, 103; suffrage 4, 106
suffrage 2–3, 31–32, 41, 105–106, 108, 110, 113, 118; American Woman Suffrage Association 105–106; National Woman Suffrage Association 105–105; *see also* woman's rights movement; *The Liberator* 33, 48–49, 54, 71; Thirteenth-Amendment 102; true woman/womanhood 59–60, 65, 71, 109

Water Cure 75, 77–78, 80, 83, 85, 87, 89, 101, 114; Battleboro, VT Water Cure 75–78; Gleason Sanitarium 114; Round Hill Water Cure 85
westward expansion 3, 42, 63
Western Female Institute 31, 33, 39, 41, 55, 57, 61
Woman's Rights Movement 46, 55, 67, 71–73, 106, 109; *see also* suffrage
Woodhull, Victoria 107–114